GILBERT & GEORGE

LONDON PICTURES

THE GILBERT & GEORGE CENTRE

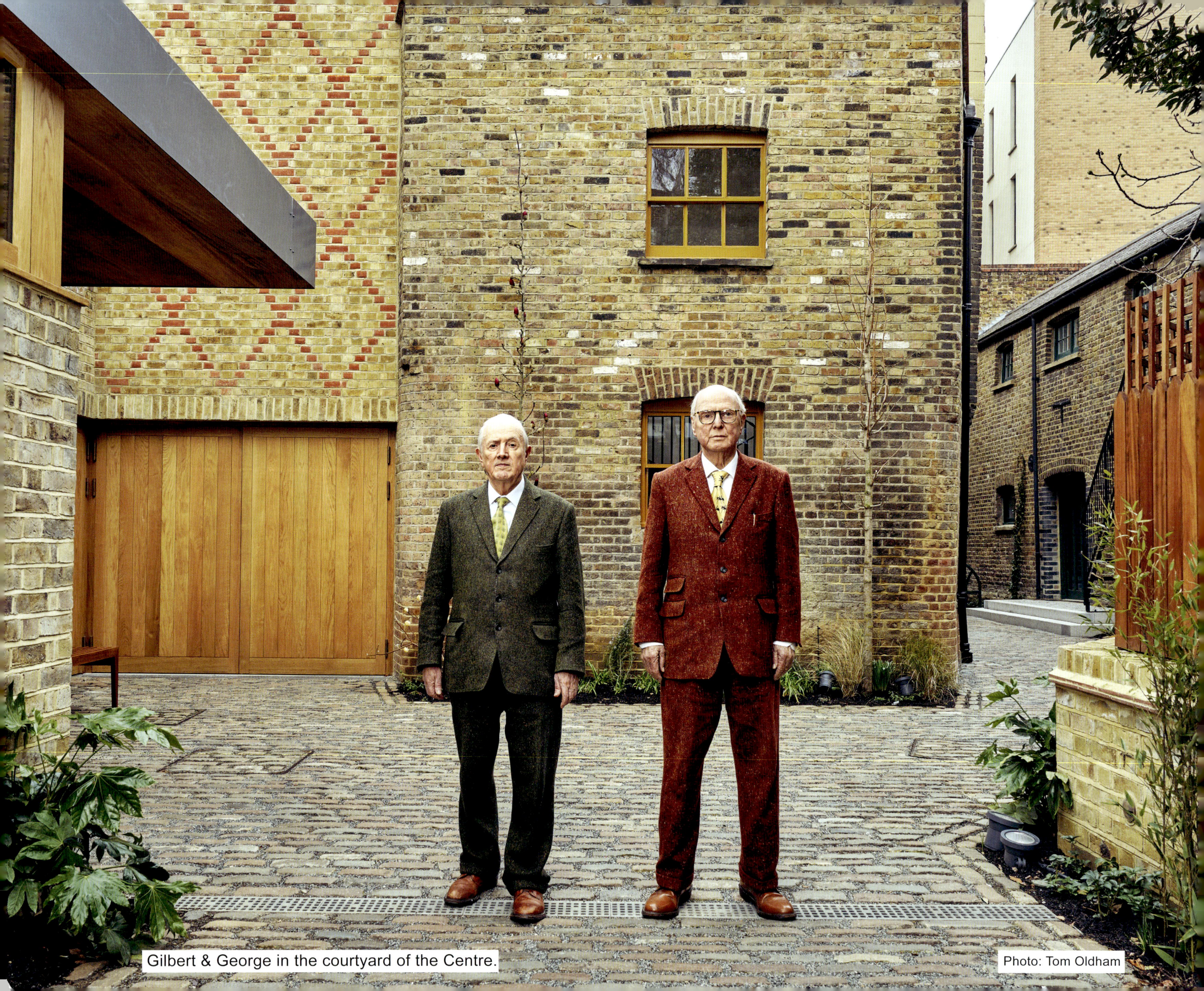

Gilbert & George in the courtyard of the Centre.

GILBERT & GEORGE

LONDON PICTURES

THE GILBERT & GEORGE CENTRE

5A Heneage Street, London E1 5LJ

2024

GILBERT & GEORGE
LONDON PICTURES 2011

Michael Bracewell

'... Gazing fearfully at the huge town before them, as if foreboding that their misery there would be but as a drop of water in the sea, or as a grain of sea-sand on the shore… Food for the hospitals, the churchyards, the prisons, the river, fever, madness, vice, and death – they passed on to the monster, roaring in the distance, and were lost.'

Charles Dickens – *Dombey and Son* (1846–48)

Throughout their art, with unwavering constancy, the vision and presence of Gilbert & George have seemed to permeate the very pores of London – the city in which they have lived and worked together since 1967. So intense is their empathy, as artists, with the streets and buildings and atmosphere, the sleepless thoroughfares and anonymous presences, the institutions and detritus and imprints of history, the strangeness and newness and dereliction of London, that they seem in their art to both haunt the city – as tireless themselves as ghosts – and to be a living part of its fabric, melding or drifting or watching, through shabby streets, polished concrete or soot-blackened brick.

In the 292 LONDON PICTURES, their extent created from the meticulous sifting and classification, by subject, of 3,712 posters, produced daily and weekly by various London newspapers, the presence of Gilbert & George has now become overtly and determinedly spirit-like – as though the artists were psychic manifestations of the city itself, its sense of place and history. The LONDON PICTURES comprise both a directory of quotidian urban human behaviour – revealing and shocking and violent, in all its sluggish or volatile momentum – and as such the city's moral portrait: an unflinching audit of modern western society's relationship to itself, stripped of rhetoric or intellectual disguise.

For these newspaper posters – this assault on reason and calm by announcements of violence, passion, misery and greed – articulate what might be termed London's nervous system: the impulses, instincts, reflexes, tics, surges and sensitivities of an illimitable torrent of human existence. Such naked feelings have always been both the subject and temper of the art of Gilbert & George, just as those same emotions and sensations, their actions and their historical consequences, have shaped the city's body, and kept its sentience alert. The LONDON PICTURES, therefore, can be seen as containing the cumulative force and intensity of the art of Gilbert & George to date. They might also mark a point when Gilbert & George, through the transformative agency of their art, become like spirits of London – a state achieved, in their art and its creations, through their intense immersion in the stuff of the city, and their identification, as witnesses and moral seers, with the cycles of life and death that it contains.

Gilbert: All the posters that we collected are from London – that is how these LONDON PICTURES began. And all the subjects are from London, and around the world.

George: We always thought that we were trying to do London pictures with *Red Morning* and so forth – but they never became specifically about London in that way; it was always edging around the subject. But then these posters enabled us to address those subjects that one connects with London: the city of murder and sex and disaster and burning buildings.

Gilbert: For years we have said that we never want to be anywhere else. London is the most important part of our inspiration. It is all that surrounds us. And so we have been able to include all this remarkable surface of thoughts and feelings that we find in these posters – you wouldn't be able to paint a picture like that. There are so many layers in these new pictures, which you wouldn't be able to do in a painting.

George: We can address those subjects that otherwise would be almost impossible. To make a big picture called *Pervert*, for instance – to be able to address that subject.

Gilbert: It feels like Dickens – he walked London and saw these things: the suicides, the rapes… These posters show the western world inside us all: it's like taking London and putting it inside an MRI scanner. And it is also like a universal diary of London. We have always felt that it takes a while for a subject, or even a building, to really speak to us. It may take years even; but then it is as though these things come to life and speak to us – and we can make art from it.

The LONDON PICTURES seem to consolidate a vision and a journey that the artists began over fifty years ago. The cyclone of feelings that they convey with such force – as though the low roar of an angry storm, rising and falling, could be felt through the newspaper media of words and images – seems summoned from the depths of an ancient and exhausted restlessness; that from the actuality of news headlines, brutal, blunt, absurd, there resonates a vision of the city as Gilbert & George have known and traversed it, drawing upon its energy, dreams and trauma as though from a palette of human feeling – recognised and employed since the beginnings of their art.

It is not that the acts and events announced by these posters are sensational and unusual; rather, the opposite: it is their regularity that shocks – the routine of horror and misery, its turbulence all pervading, its reliability known; but its reality usually unseen. How did Gilbert & George come to know this city, and enable themselves to merge with its torpor, vexed energy, battered streets and magnificence?

Having met at St Martin's School of Art in 1967, on London's busy Charing Cross Road, the two young artists chose to become separate from their teachers and peers, preferring to explore the vastness and mystery of the city around them. Here lay the inspiration for their life's work as one artist, Gilbert & George. Almost immediately they knew and declared that they were Living Sculptures – that they, Gilbert & George, were their art. They dressed soberly and correctly, as smartly as their circumstances allowed. They were polite and friendly to all whom they met. They worked from dawn until dusk, every day, to turn the intensity of their feelings and their experiences into art, and to make a place where they could live. They roamed the city and London absorbed them – in exact proportion to the manner in which they absorbed London.

Gilbert: It is to do with our loneliness – our loneliness when we started our art. The feeling of our first book *Side By Side* (1971), and going into the *Dark Shadow* (1974) of loneliness in a different way – all this stuff is there, already, I really believe it: broken bottles; postcards of unhappy landscapes. And then with pictures DUSTY CORNERS (1975) and DEAD BOARDS (1976) – this atmosphere… It was not the street, but it was the loneliness of the world. And with these LONDON PICTURES we are able to show an extraordinary townscape of London.

George: Bleak and empty and desolate…

Gilbert: Even the trees in our pictures are yearning for something. And even when we made the COSMOLOGICAL PICTURES (1989), it was like a yearning for an ideal dream world. You never see the world for what it is, you see it through your own brain – different for everyone: happy, unhappy, the struggle of life. And with these LONDON PICTURES, it's all real, not fake – that's what we like.

Gilbert & George had settled in the East End of London, first in Wilkes Street, and then Fournier Street – at that time a dangerous and derelict district, hard by Liverpool Street Station. To the west of them, the old City of London maintained its enclosed, medieval world – Italianate banks and counting houses, dim courtyards, smoky dining rooms and dark pubs; a district that between the 1980s and the present would suddenly accelerate its modernity – becoming ultra-modern and stateless, the hub of the biggest and wealthiest financial centre in the world; and around which, like a dirty tide, the renovation-encrusted buildings of Edwardian and Victorian London retained their cowed and battered air.

Around Spitalfields, where the artists lived, the darkling eighteenth century streets seemed to lie densely scattered, like bleached and broken bones; and in the tall, high-windowed houses, beyond their dismal or portentous front doors, could be found little workshops, furriers' rooms, obscure offices and businesses, store rooms, artisan studios or solitary tenants. Alternately bustling and desolate, it was a place of working men's cafes and poor families; their neighbours were market porters, tramps, immigrant workers and worshippers, and 'the meths men' – alcoholics who drank themselves to blindness and death on industrial ethanol, fumous and mauvish. It was the lingering twilight of this society that Gilbert & George would later create in their film, made in 1981, *The World of Gilbert & George*.

But within these surroundings, Gilbert & George discovered an aspect of London that might have seemed unchanged for a hundred years. Always researching the history of London, the artists would read that in 1869, J. Ewing Ritchie had pronounced:

'The swells in the Park, the millers in Mark Lane, the graziers in the new cattle market, the Jews in Houndsditch or Holywell Street, the prim pale lads in the City, the sailors at Shadwell, and Deptford and Wapping, the German sugar-bakers in Whitechapel, the Chinese opium smokers in Tiger Bay – really form distinct communities as any Red Indians dwelling beyond the sunset, and the bars and of all the western stars. A large book might be written about the east of London

…' And so this East of the city would be for Gilbert & George the crucible of human feelings and behaviour – the place in which the local becomes the universal:

George: We have always said that when you see the church in one of our pictures, it is not the church in Fournier Street – it's the church inside you. Because for or against the church, we all know what it means.

Gilbert: And in every interview we ever gave, we always said that the centre of the universe is Liverpool Street Station.

George: And that if a space ship was arriving from outer space, and they had five minutes to interview people about life on Earth, the city that they would go to is London. There would be no use going to Zurich – that's typical planet Earth circa 1937. Whereas London is Today.

Historically, the East End of London had not only been poor, to the point of destitute, but also home to society's outcasts, victims and criminal classes. Those who slipped beneath the surface of London's brutally strong currents and rip tides could find themselves dragged under, to the shabby streets and missions and hostels to be found around Shoreditch and Whitechapel. The houses and streets were both sanctuary and prison, an enclosed universe, to many of their inhabitants – and daily witness to the extremes of life as much as its drear momentum: intoxication, struggle and violence, prayer and hope and work and misery were the commonplace heaving and groaning of this dank section of the urban machine.

Gilbert: There is something of our art from 1980 in these LONDON PICTURES – when we made pictures such as ALDGATE and SPITALFIELDS and FOURNIER STREET.

George: The general educated opinion of these pictures at that time was 'Why on Earth would you bring these wretched disgusting subjects of this vile part of London into the gallery? We know what goes on down there. We don't need to see pictures of it…' We were accused of 'snooping on low-life' when we made THE DIRTY WORDS (1977) pictures. But Dickens did that, didn't he? And we're living in the middle of it here anyway – to call it 'snooping' is absurd.

The LONDON PICTURES derive a great part of their impact and intensity from the directness and unchanged immediacy of the newspaper posters within all but one panel of each picture. In each remaining panel, as though adding the Royal Warrant to each forensic pronouncement of outrage – for example: STAB, STAB DEATH, STABBED – can be found a different image of HM Queen Elizabeth II, taken from a coin, her countenance and profile changing with age, dented and worn through the usage of currency. There is a stark and arresting juxtaposition of this iconic likeness, potent with pomp and authority, and the alphabetical index of outrage, by subject, refined by the LONDON PICTURES. Her Majesty appears to endorse the title of each picture, providing a state colophon to their vision of modern London; and by doing so become implicated in the society and morality that they describe. The words 'IT'S WRITTEN ALL OVER THEM' beneath the legend 'A LONDON PICTURE' propose that these headlines cannot help but reveal what we as a society have become capable of, and have allowed to happen. Behind modern urban society's veneer of respectability and order, volatility and suffering are constant.

The great Victorian visionary and critic John Ruskin also reported on the lives of East London's suffering, direct from their own testaments, in his three lectures *Sesame and*

Lilies written in 1867. The atmosphere of the supernatural is present – not in Ruskin's thesis or prose, but in the intensity of atmosphere and strangeness within the reported testaments. Taken from a *Daily Telegraph* newspaper of that year, Ruskin recounts the coroner's court hearing of the case of a deceased workman – first blinded by close work in poor light, and finally starving to death. Like Dickens, in his accusatory political essay 'The Parish', Ruskin was appalled by the callousness of the Parish as a social service. These abject conditions are matched by the surrealism of the witness's language – as he confesses to preferring starvation and death, rather than entering the parish workhouse:

'A Juror: "You are dying of starvation yourself, and you ought to go into the house [workhouse] until summer." Witness: "If we went in we should die. When we come out in the summer we should be like people dropped from the sky. No one would know us, and we would not even have a room."'

As seems to lie behind the posters of the contemporary London newspapers, it is the routine and regularity of this suffering within the metropolis that both appalls and gives rise to a form of semantic strangeness. Beyond the statistic and the legal investigation of the death, there stretch the sensitivities of a human life, and the interconnectedness of that life to others. And yet the monumental significance of that life and its death becomes absorbed into the bureaucratic, daily flow of the city's workings. It is the acknowledgement of such an assimilation, the moral drama that exists beneath the typographical shorthand of a newspaper poster, that the LONDON PICTURES reveal – the 'moral dimension' that Gilbert & George must feel within a subject, in order to transpose that dimension into their art, and make it available to the viewer.

Such has always been their mission. Early on, in their neat suits, the best that they could manage, Gilbert & George worked tirelessly at their art – walking the streets, day and night, to the furthest edges and deepest recesses of London, always discovering and experiencing new feelings and new impressions. And soon they knew that in the few streets around Fournier Street – this urban whirlpool – they could find all of the qualities, good and bad, that comprise the modern human condition. The voice of London became, for the artists, what they called its 'moral dimension' – sometimes made eloquent through the traces, records, detritus and excreta left behind by the passage and lives of anonymous strangers; on other occasions newly found in familiar sites, buildings or trees. To reveal and explore this moral dimension has been the subject and main purpose of all of the art of Gilbert & George.

George: We always say that we take images of a subject again and again, until we find the moral dimension – and then it speaks to us. Like we took images outside buildings of lace curtains – and we didn't know why. Then we took more, and we suddenly realised that these curtains were like the house's burka; they serve the same function – the people in the house can look out, but we can't look in. And in that moment we were able to use these images in the new LONDON PICTURES. We wouldn't have been able to use them until we knew what they mean to us.

Gilbert: These posters are amazing realism – an amazingly intense vision of a city. London is the most on-edge city in the world – people want to come here from all over world. I am sure that we are part of the dark side of East London – we wouldn't go to the West End to take an image. We know that misery is fascinating. That's human life – hidden suffering.

And in some ways we are exposing what is going on inside people's minds. We have to fill our brains with a density of a particular image, in order to work out what it means to us, and what it might mean to the viewer. And sometimes, very rarely, a single image might take us off in a whole new direction.

George: I am sure that when we made the picture 'NEWS', in 2004, which includes images of a newspaper poster, we didn't know or plan or think that one day we would make a whole group of pictures based on newspaper posters.

Gilbert: It was later that we became interested in that whole world of subjects like suicide, rape, killing, murder, OAPs… It became like a new world – subjects that you wouldn't normally be able to use in art; how would you use this stuff in art? Only because it is written down and combined with these layers: of brick walls, and us melting into them or into trees… It becomes like a vision of London – a certain London that exists…

The scope of the LONDON PICTURES is epic, and derives from the manner in which each picture, to a greater extent, automatically 'creates itself' as a consequence of the means by which Gilbert & George have classified and catalogued the newspaper headline posters that comprise each text-based panel. Thus the 292 LONDON PICTURES have been determined in size and title by the mathematical and alphabetical refinement, by subject, of the 3,712 posters that were stolen and accumulated by the artists over many years. As they were collecting these posters, Gilbert & George had no inkling or premonition as to what their eventual purpose would be.

Gilbert: At first we just had posters, which we had stolen over the years – a massive amount. We would walk each day over to Liverpool Street, and one of us would buy a Mars Bar while the other stole the poster.

George: We didn't realise how many we had collected – we thought it was just a couple of hundred posters.

Gilbert: When we counted them, there were 3,712. Then, just before Christmas 2010, we started laying them down by subject on the studio floor – and it was amazing.

George: Many of the posters have more than one subject; so it was like a 'four layer' sort-out. For instance, within the subject heading 'KILL', there is 'boy', 'girl', 'woman', 'man' – so we had to adjust the piles. Subjects such as 'STAB' and 'DEATH' have too many variants, and so we had to make a decision as to which to keep. And so for instance there is a picture called 'STAB' and a picture called 'STAB DEATH' – within the larger subject area of stabbings.

Gilbert: We had to be able to break it down into a system – beginning alphabetically by subject. For those subject groups which were too big, we looked to see what other words occurred, and whether we could make a picture from those – secondary subjects. We also have to leave one panel free, bottom right, for the title – so to make an eight-part picture we needed seven posters that included the word referring to its subject. So from the posters themselves, sorted in this system by word and subject, we knew the title of a picture and how big it was. For each picture we made a folder, with the title, and all the images relating to that picture.

George: This system is also very revealing. For instance, when we isolate the word 'LONDON' we find that the other frequent word within that subject area is 'MONEY'. For 'LOVER' we have fifteen posters, and within those headlines we also find: 'KILLED', 'MURDER', 'MONEY', 'DIES',

'HACKED TO DEATH'… Whereas you would have thought that 'LOVER' would be quite a nice list, wouldn't you? The simple system when we were first sifting the posters was: nothing pleasant. And a friend said that surely there must be plenty of pleasant subjects – but they must be invisible to us, because I don't remember seeing any.

And thus, from the 3,712 stolen posters, the alphabetical list of LONDON PICTURES began to create itself through an almost automatic process: ACCUSED, ADDICT, ADDICTS, ANGEL, ARMED, ARREST, ARREST STRAIGHT… A further nuance was added to the composition and titling of the LONDON PICTURES by the distinction between those posters printed in a thicker, cursive script (like hand-written capital letters) and those printed in more etiolated sans serif capital letters. The latter were always denoted, as a suffix to the title, STRAIGHT. In this, Gilbert & George were both distinguishing the two typefaces, but also making a play on the use of 'straight' as slang for 'heterosexual'. Their point was that the continued highlighting of 'gay' society was irrelevant, outmoded and divisive; for example, why distinguish between 'gay' and 'straight' marriage, rather than simply referring to 'marriage'? The inclusive aspect of the subjects described by the LONDON PICTURES – its democracy of events and social types – was a feature that they found particularly interesting.

The viewer's experience of each picture begins, perhaps, with the manner in which the images of Gilbert & George – stern, impassive, staring, or glimpsed on a street as though photo-journalistically – take their places within the background of poster-based panels. They are always depicted in a figurative, unmanipulated form, and yet their presence is otherworldly and ghostlike. They seem to stare towards the viewer in a manner that is simultaneously accusatory and mute, knowing and impassive, sentient and vacant. Elsewhere they are seen as though from afar – even the sunlight on a street adding somehow to their strangeness and solitude, their sense of being both within the present and a visitor to it.

In this the artists consolidate, artistically, what might be seen as their 'psychic' constitution as Living Sculptures and the authors of *Side By Side* (1971) and *Dark Shadow* (1974) – their place as eternal outsiders, sleepless wanderers of the city, urban seers, 'super-tramps', isolated, dispossessed, solitary: finding a spiritual home (as young artists) beneath a railway arch; later, becoming monstrous versions of themselves, crazed and gesticulating like mad sentinels. Within the LONDON PICTURES they appear as fragments, reflections or transparent versions of themselves: their edges are sometimes blurred, or their bodies merge into whiteness; at times their heads are distorted, but not as mutants – rather, as presences just glimpsed on the street by chance, that disappear as soon as they are recognised. There is neither sadness nor anger about their presence: rather a sense of eternal patience or impassive watchfulness – a quality that has also been constant through the art of Gilbert & George.

In relation to the LONDON PICTURES, the artists had also, serendipitously, come across the writings of Lord Dowding – Air Chief Marshall and Commander-in-Chief of the Royal Air Force during the Battle of Britain. Subsequent to winning the Battle of Britain, Dowding – perhaps traumatised by strain and exhaustion, perhaps not – became increasingly interested in spiritualism, and in the induction of spirits into the afterlife. From these interests he wrote several books, all of which have been of great interest to Gilbert & George. His particular concept of ghosts and spirits, therefore, informed an aspect of the artists' depiction of themselves within the LONDON PICTURES. But it is the manner in which the presence of Gilbert & George, within these pictures, becomes synonymous with the intense and particular atmosphere of the city that is paramount: how they depict themselves as ghostlike extensions of London's dark, brooding or near-electrical sentience – emanations from a numinous geography.

Gilbert: The layers in the LONDON PICTURES melt together – it's extraordinary. It is like spirits of London – walking the streets. But it is also by accident; we noticed that some of the images looked like spirits, and then we started to read Lord Dowding's books about ghosts. Spirits can be in your brain, too – memories and dreams can be three dimensional, as can the very intense atmosphere on a street or from a building.

George: We like to think that we, along with the viewer, are all complicit in how we have made the world. We wanted each picture to 'decide itself' – the same way that a day decides itself.

George: We always liked the idea of Dowding, because, like Bomber Harris, he divides opinion. He won the Battle of Britain, which stopped a Nazi invasion of this country, which would have changed the course of history. But there are still people who think that there shouldn't be a statue to him. We also liked the idea that he had parties in his headquarters with the killed pilots, who were dressed as they were when they were killed – he wrote at great length about that. You can argue about this forever, but he certainly wasn't a liar.

Gilbert: He was so unhappy and obsessed that these young people were dead – after just one flight maybe – that he started seeing them coming back alive…

George: We were taking pictures of ourselves in the yard, and then blanked out with white everything except the figure and a bit of yard, or holes in us… And so you saw aspects of us. It is not an obvious thing, which we like as well – but more mysterious, like the Dowding boys.

Gilbert: It made us as though we were melting into the surroundings – a 'spirit image'; or like the wartime Powell & Pressburger film [*A Matter of Life and Death*] about the young airman caught between life and death.

The remaining visual elements of the LONDON PICTURES are pared down and literal: streets, house-fronts, bricks, net curtains, car window reflections. The colours are refined to black and white, red and flesh colour. This palette is also the consequence of the automatic formulation of the pictures, and the removal by the artists of any conscious compositional process or decision-making.

George: We knew we wanted them to be black and white, and that red is the most expressive colour for the title. And the only other thing in all of the pictures is the human presence, so we added flesh colour.

Gilbert: A black and white image can just speak more. And the accident of the aesthetic, we like very much. In some ways, we have taken the process of composition away. We didn't change anything.

George: And we decided that we would not violate the posters in the LONDON PICTURES in any way. We didn't want the images we took and used to be consciously 'good', technically. They should just be like something you see on your way to breakfast in the morning, or on your way home in the evening. They are automatic in the sense that they are not concentrated – no thinking or planning at all.

Gilbert: We simply needed an atmosphere to complete the picture.

George: If someone comes down the street, you maybe don't know who they are, where they've come from or where they're going. And the images can be like that, also. They will make their own life.

Gilbert: We create a visual spirit – like an atmosphere from a time or day; it is not composed… We wanted to be taken over by the spirit of it.

George: But strangely, we think that we have made very moving images. We only realised that at the end. We lived the process of making these pictures, more than any others we have made: of being with them, alone, in them.

The LONDON PICTURES can be seen as the incendiary conflation of an automatic, classification-based process, and a deep excursion into the psychic and emotional territory that has been pioneered by the art of Gilbert & George. In the past, the artists have spoken of how in order to create they must maintain an absolute balance, in themselves, between technical control and 'crazed' or 'dead-headed' psychology. The LONDON PICTURES can be seen as a monumental testament to this creative dichotomy: wherein the 'self-deciding' compositional process of the pictures is matched by a deeper and deeper advance, by the artists, into the gravitational field of atmosphere, place, time and feelings. It is the territory of Dickens' *Night Walks* – in which the secrets of all London must seem to lie bare before his undefended, vulnerable but all-seeing gaze: a place beyond sadness, or death or event, where the only continuum is the life energy of the city, flowing without pause or emotion, eternally, indifferent to individual human destiny.

George: This is the great adventure of western Greco Roman, Judaeo-Christian secularist society, always trying to move forward, always under attack. Everything playing its part in an onward and ongoing gradual improvement.

Gilbert: Trying to understand one another – that is surely the most important thing? I think it is the balance to survive. The skies don't change because we have murders in the street.

George: Maybe the LONDON PICTURES are the local version of that.

Gilbert: They tell an amazing story. That is what we love – they are the cries of London: the street cries of London.

George: And they are also the doorway into this amazing world – of misery, unhappiness and shame.

The interviews with Gilbert & George were conducted by the author during November and December 2011.

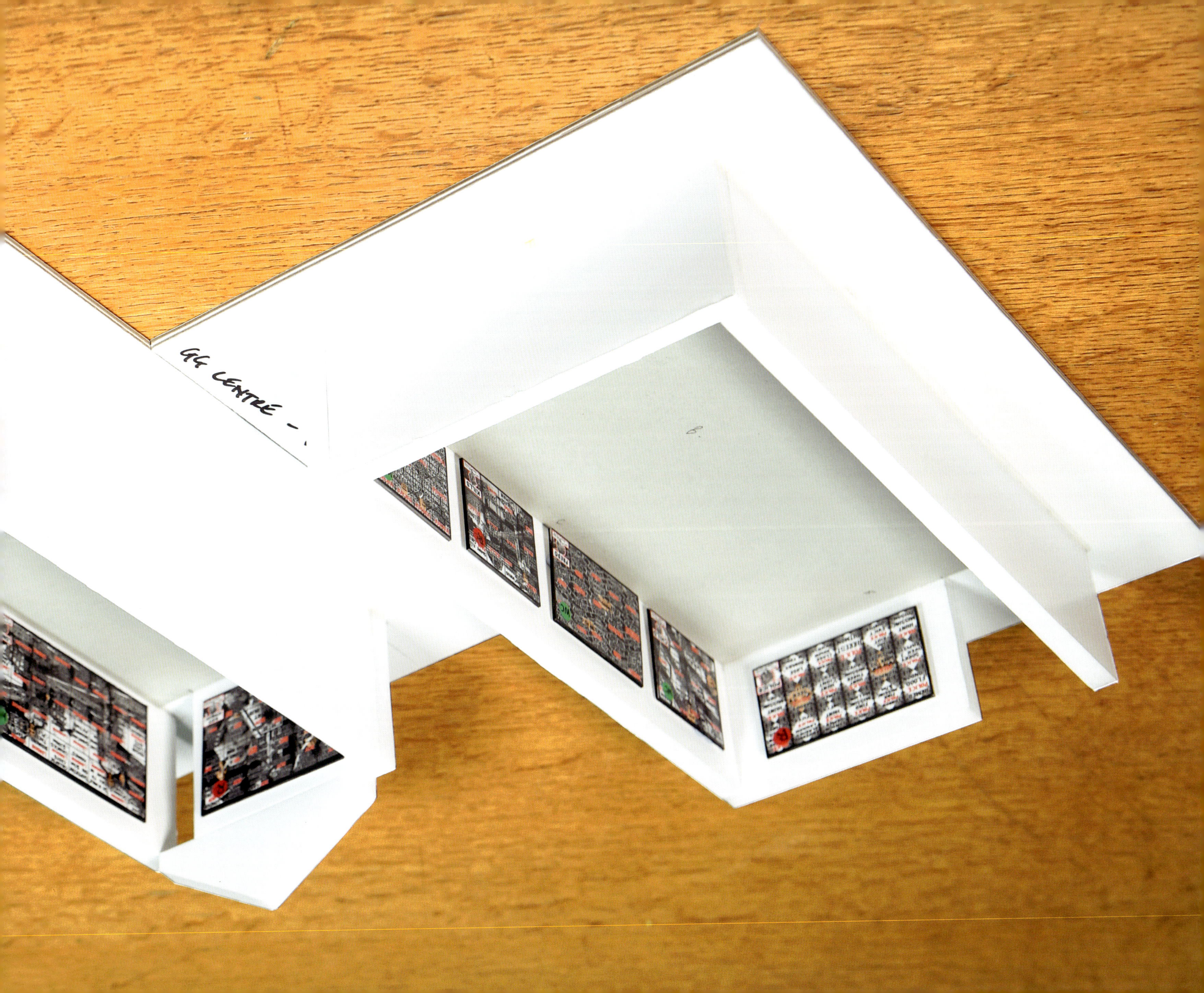

GG CENTRE -

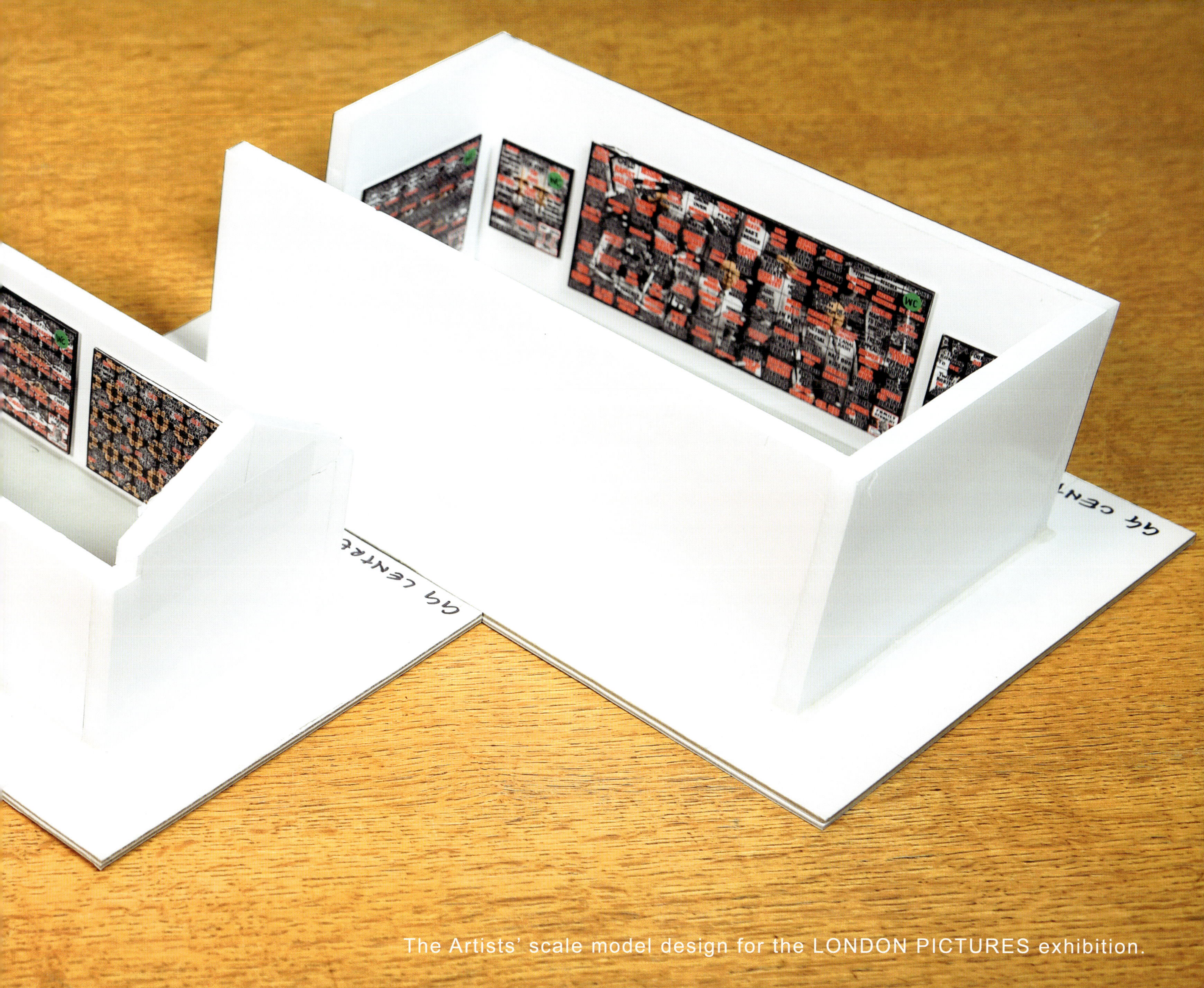

The Artists' scale model design for the LONDON PICTURES exhibition.

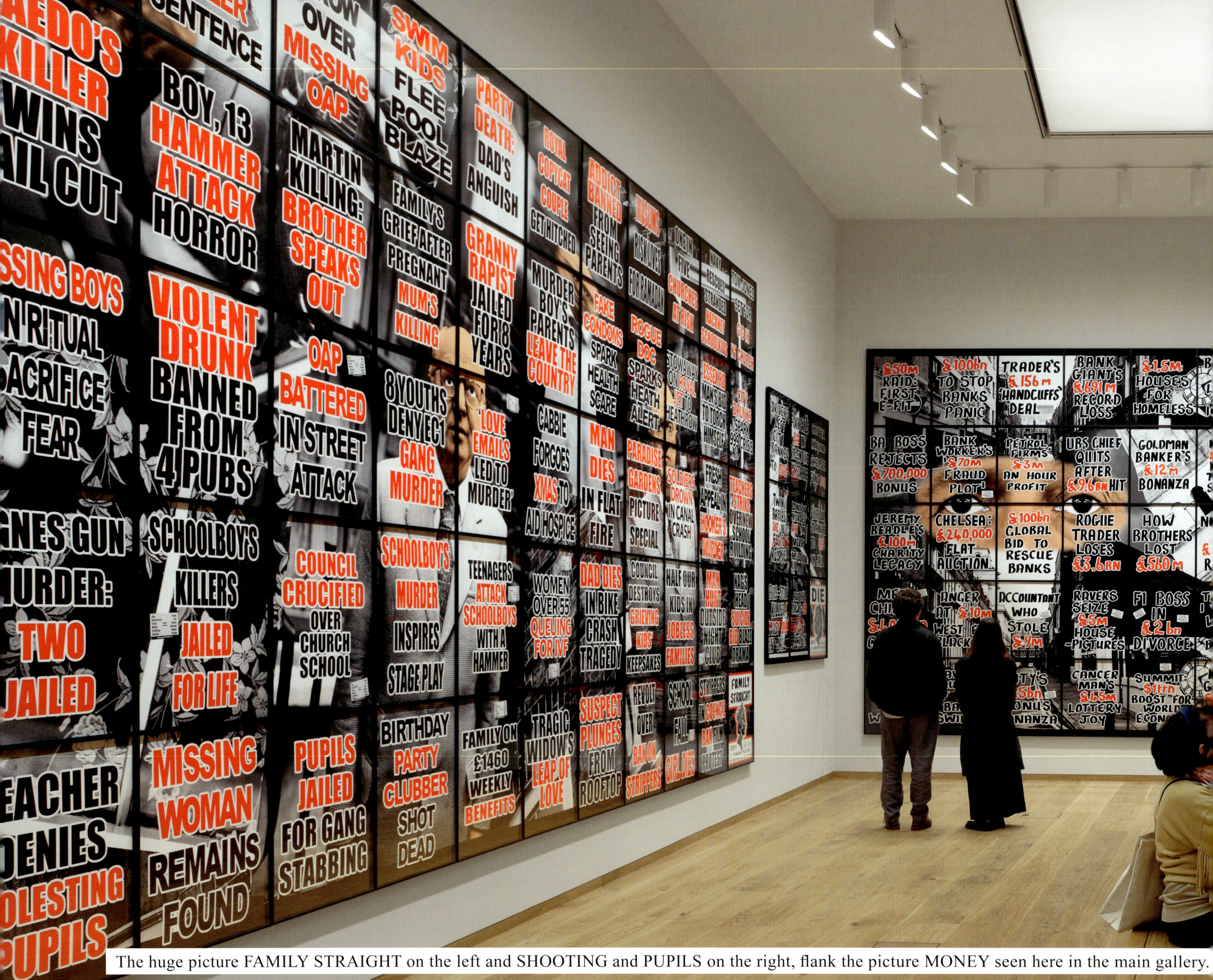

The huge picture FAMILY STRAIGHT on the left and SHOOTING and PUPILS on the right, flank the picture MONEY seen here in the main gallery.

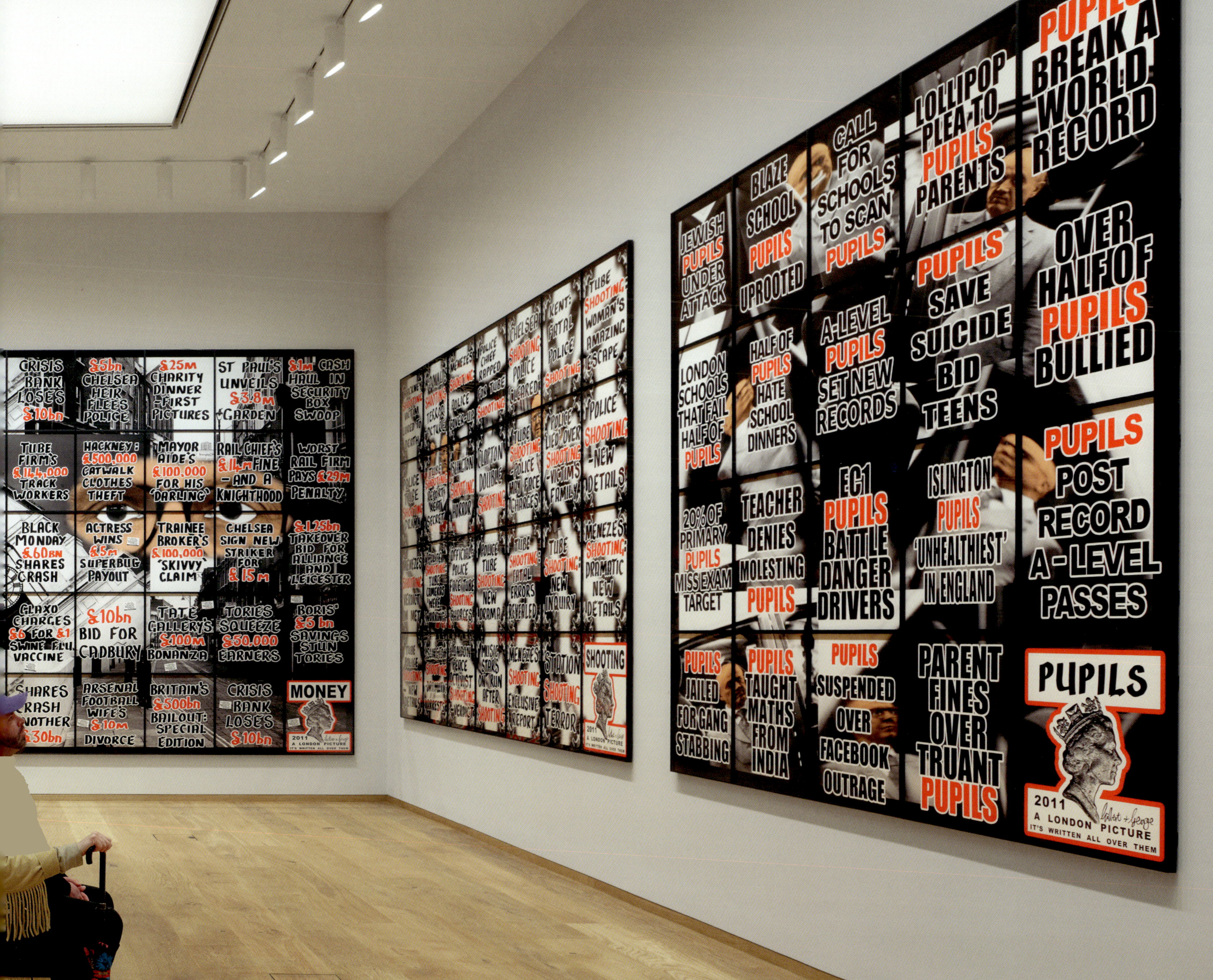
PUPILS BREAK A WORLD RECORD
LOLLIPOP PLEA TO PUPILS PARENTS
CALL FOR SCHOOLS TO SCAN PUPILS
BLAZE SCHOOL PUPILS UPROOTED
JEWISH PUPILS UNDER ATTACK
OVER HALF OF PUPILS BULLIED
PUPILS SAVE SUICIDE BID TEENS
A-LEVEL PUPILS SET NEW RECORDS
HALF OF PUPILS HATE SCHOOL DINNERS
LONDON SCHOOLS THAT FAIL HALF OF PUPILS
PUPILS POST RECORD A-LEVEL PASSES
ISLINGTON PUPILS 'UNHEALTHIEST' IN ENGLAND
EC1 PUPILS BATTLE DANGER DRIVERS
TEACHER DENIES MOLESTING PUPILS
20% OF PRIMARY PUPILS MISS EXAM TARGET
PARENT FINES OVER TRUANT PUPILS
PUPILS SUSPENDED OVER FACEBOOK OUTRAGE
PUPILS TAUGHT MATHS FROM INDIA
PUPILS JAILED FOR GANG STABBING
PUPILS
2011 A LONDON PICTURE
IT'S WRITTEN ALL OVER THEM
CRISIS BANK LOSES £10bn
£5bn CHELSEA HEIR FLEES POLICE
£25m CHARITY DINNER FIRST PICTURES
ST PAULS UNVEILS £3.8m GARDEN
£1m CASH HAUL IN SECURITY BOX SWOOP
TUBE FIRM'S £164,000 TRACK WORKERS
HACKNEY: £500,000 CATWALK CLOTHES THEFT
MAYOR AIDE'S £100,000 FOR HIS 'DARLING'
RAIL CHIEF'S £1m FINE — AND A KNIGHTHOOD
WORST RAIL FIRM PAYS £29M PENALTY
BLACK MONDAY £60m SHARES CRASH
ACTRESS WINS £5m SUPERBUG PAYOUT
TRAINEE BROKER'S £100,000 'SKIVVY' CLAIM
CHELSEA SIGN NEW STRIKER FOR £15m
£1.25bn TAKEOVER BID FOR ALLIANCE AND LEICESTER
GLAXO CHARGES £6 FOR £1 SWINE FLU VACCINE
£10bn BID FOR CADBURY
TATE GALLERY'S £100m BONANZA
TORIES SQUEEZE £50,000 EARNERS
BORIS' £5bn SAVINGS STUN TORIES
SHARES CRASH ANOTHER £30bn
ARSENAL FOOTBALL WIFE'S £10m DIVORCE
BRITAIN'S £800bn BAILOUT: SPECIAL EDITION
CRISIS BANK LOSES £10bn
MONEY
2011 A LONDON PICTURE
IT'S WRITTEN ALL OVER THEM
SHOOTING
SHOOTING
STATION SHOOTING TERROR
SHOOTING

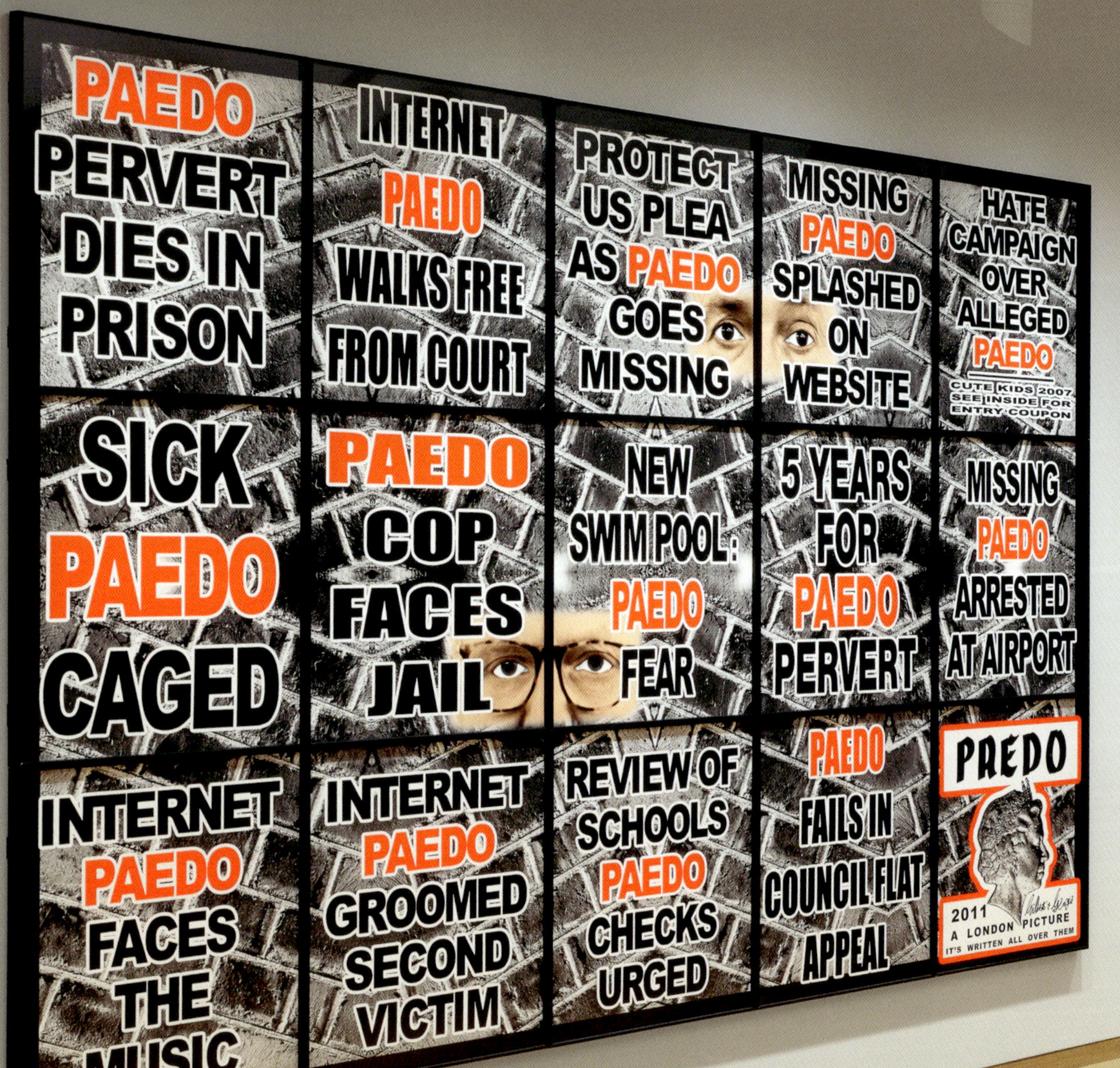

PAEDO PERVERT DIES IN PRISON
INTERNET PAEDO WALKS FREE FROM COURT
PROTECT US PLEA AS PAEDO GOES MISSING
MISSING PAEDO SPLASHED ON WEBSITE
HATE CAMPAIGN OVER ALLEGED PAEDO
CUTE KIDS 2007 SEE INSIDE FOR ENTRY COUPON
SICK PAEDO CAGED
PAEDO COP FACES JAIL
NEW SWIM POOL: PAEDO FEAR
5 YEARS FOR PAEDO PERVERT
MISSING PAEDO ARRESTED AT AIRPORT
INTERNET PAEDO FACES THE MUSIC
INTERNET PAEDO GROOMED SECOND VICTIM
REVIEW OF SCHOOLS PAEDO CHECKS URGED
PAEDO FAILS IN COUNCIL FLAT APPEAL
PAEDO
2011
A LONDON PICTURE
IT'S WRITTEN ALL OVER THEM

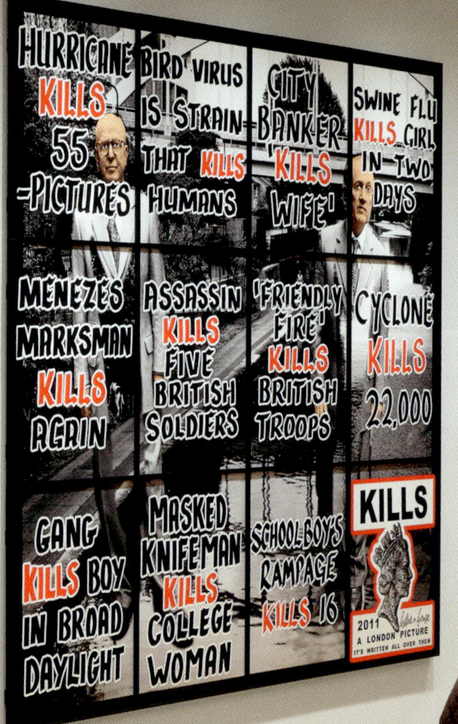

HURRICANE KILLS 55 - PICTURES
BIRD VIRUS IS STRAIN THAT KILLS HUMANS
CITY BANKER KILLS WIFE
SWINE FLU KILLS GIRL IN TWO DAYS
MENEZES MARKSMAN KILLS AGAIN
ASSASSIN KILLS FIVE BRITISH SOLDIERS
'FRIENDLY FIRE' KILLS BRITISH TROOPS
CYCLONE KILLS 22,000
GANG KILLS BOY IN BROAD DAYLIGHT
MASKED KNIFE MAN KILLS COLLEGE WOMAN
SCHOOLBOYS' RAMPAGE KILLS 16
KILLS
2011
A LONDON PICTURE
IT'S WRITTEN ALL OVER THEM

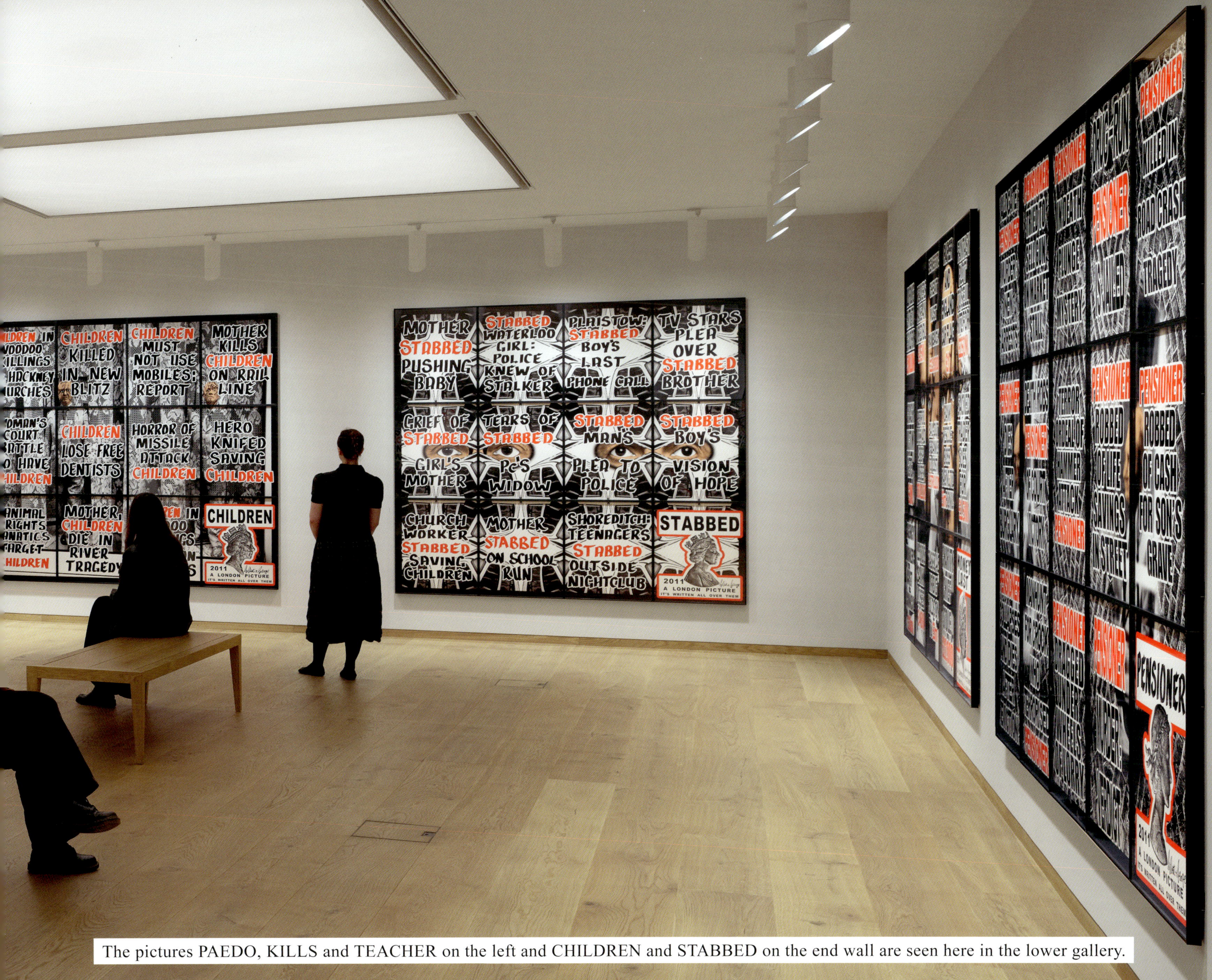

The pictures PAEDO, KILLS and TEACHER on the left and CHILDREN and STABBED on the end wall are seen here in the lower gallery.

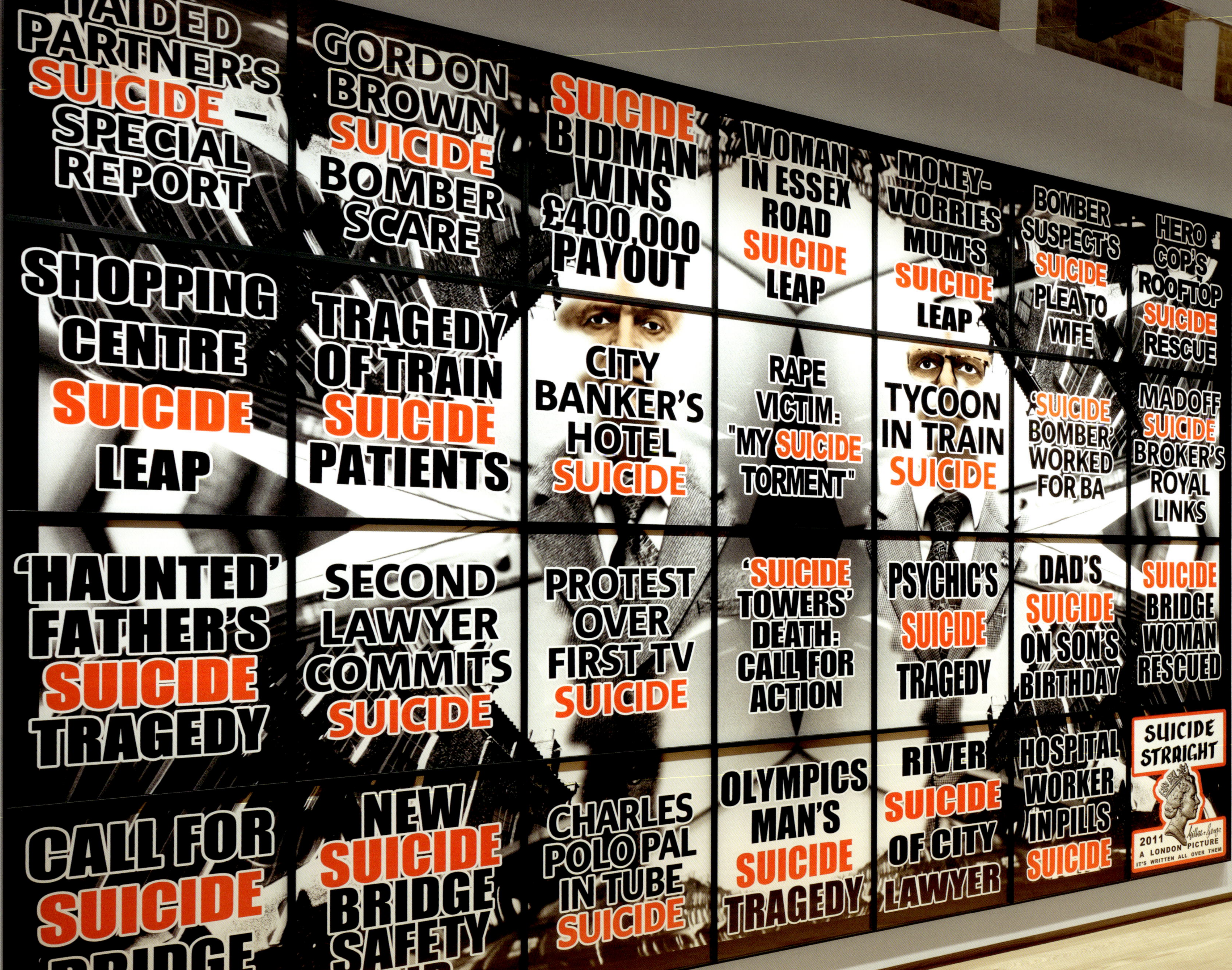
...AIDED PARTNER'S SUICIDE – SPECIAL REPORT
GORDON BROWN SUICIDE BOMBER SCARE
SUICIDE BIDIMAN WINS £400,000 PAYOUT
WOMAN IN ESSEX ROAD SUICIDE LEAP
MONEY-WORRIES MUM'S SUICIDE LEAP
BOMBER SUSPECT'S SUICIDE PLEA TO WIFE
HERO COP'S ROOFTOP SUICIDE RESCUE
SHOPPING CENTRE SUICIDE LEAP
TRAGEDY OF TRAIN SUICIDE PATIENTS
CITY BANKER'S HOTEL SUICIDE
RAPE VICTIM: "MY SUICIDE TORMENT"
TYCOON IN TRAIN SUICIDE
'SUICIDE BOMBER' WORKED FOR BA
MADOFF SUICIDE BROKER'S ROYAL LINKS
'HAUNTED' FATHER'S SUICIDE TRAGEDY
SECOND LAWYER COMMITS SUICIDE
PROTEST OVER FIRST TV SUICIDE
'SUICIDE TOWERS' DEATH: CALL FOR ACTION
PSYCHIC'S SUICIDE TRAGEDY
DAD'S SUICIDE ON SON'S BIRTHDAY
SUICIDE BRIDGE WOMAN RESCUED
CALL FOR SUICIDE BRIDGE 'COS' LINE
NEW SUICIDE BRIDGE SAFETY BID
CHARLES POLO PAL IN TUBE SUICIDE
OLYMPICS MAN'S SUICIDE TRAGEDY
RIVER SUICIDE OF CITY LAWYER
HOSPITAL WORKER IN PILLS SUICIDE
SUICIDE STRAIGHT
2011
A LONDON PICTURE
IT'S WRITTEN ALL OVER THEM

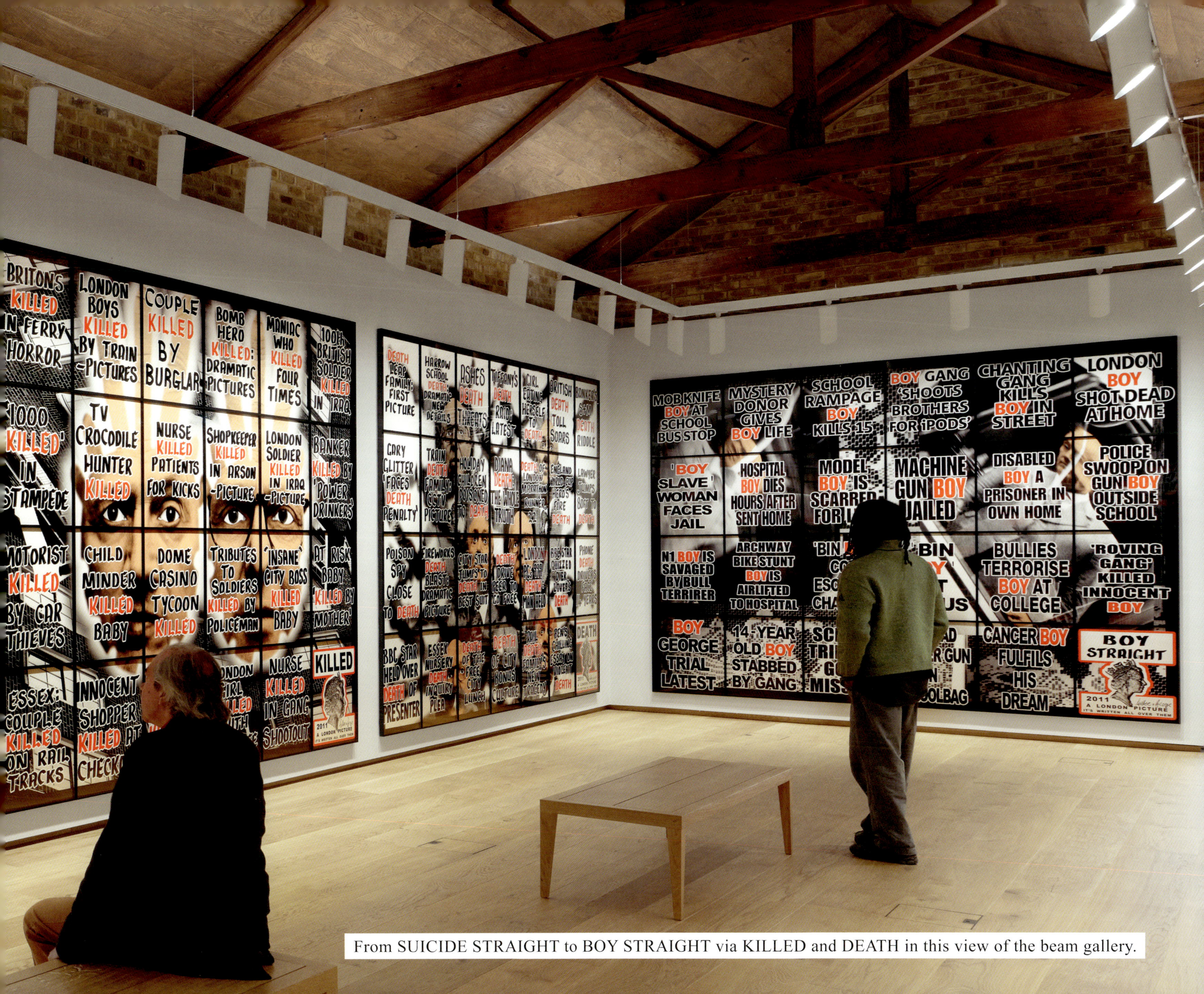

From SUICIDE STRAIGHT to BOY STRAIGHT via KILLED and DEATH in this view of the beam gallery.

THE LONDON PICTURES EXHIBITION

BOY STRAIGHT	KNIFE MURDER	SEX
CHILD	KNIFE STRAIGHT	SHOOTING
CHILDREN	LONDON	STABBED
DEATH	MONEY	STABBED TO DEATH
DIE	MONEY LAST	SUICIDE STRAIGHT
FAMILY STRAIGHT	PAEDO	TEACHER
KILL	PENSIONER	TEEN STRAIGHT
KILLED	POLICE	TERROR
KILLS	PREACHER	TOP TOTS
	PUPILS	

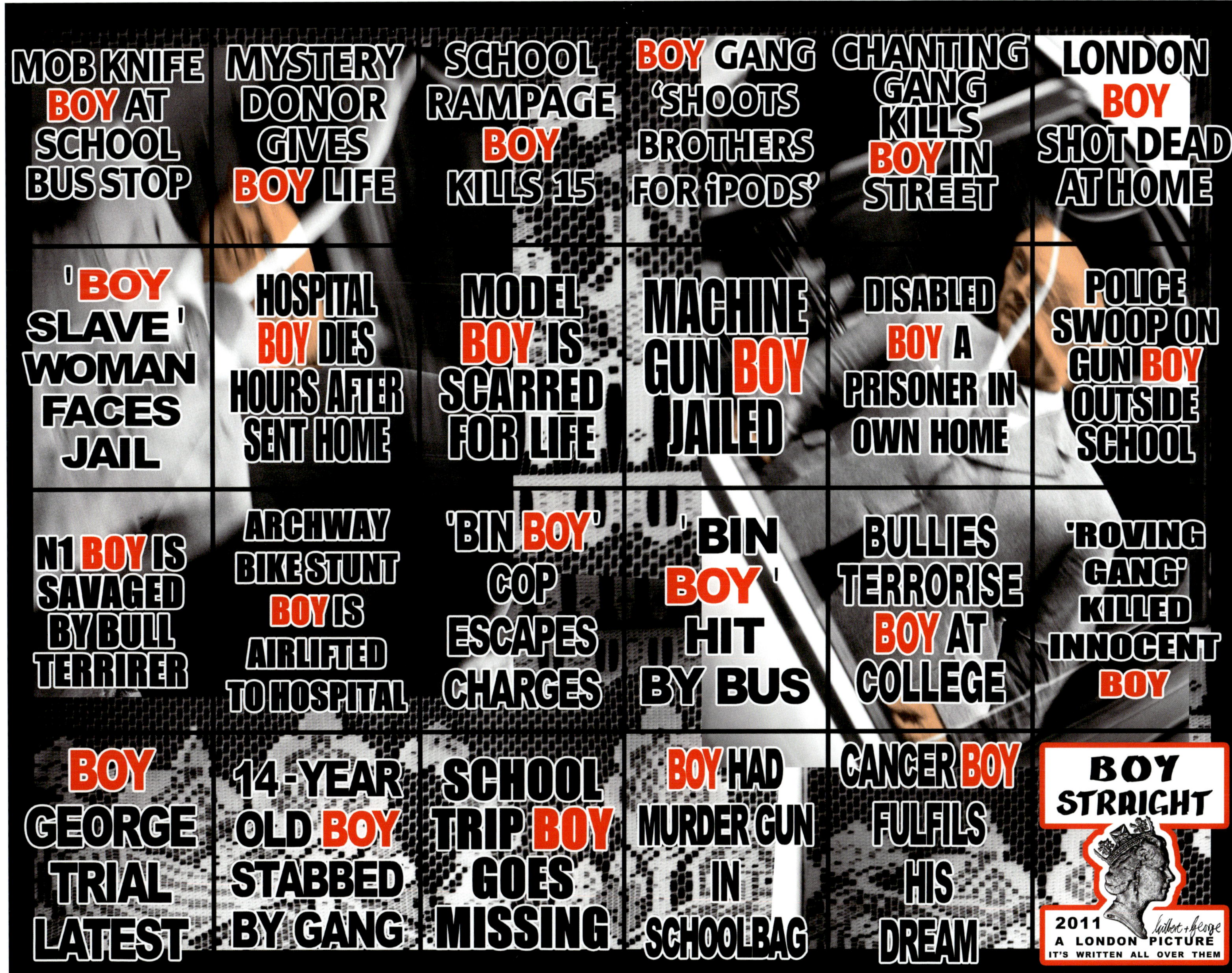

BOY STRAIGHT. 2011. 302 x 381 cm

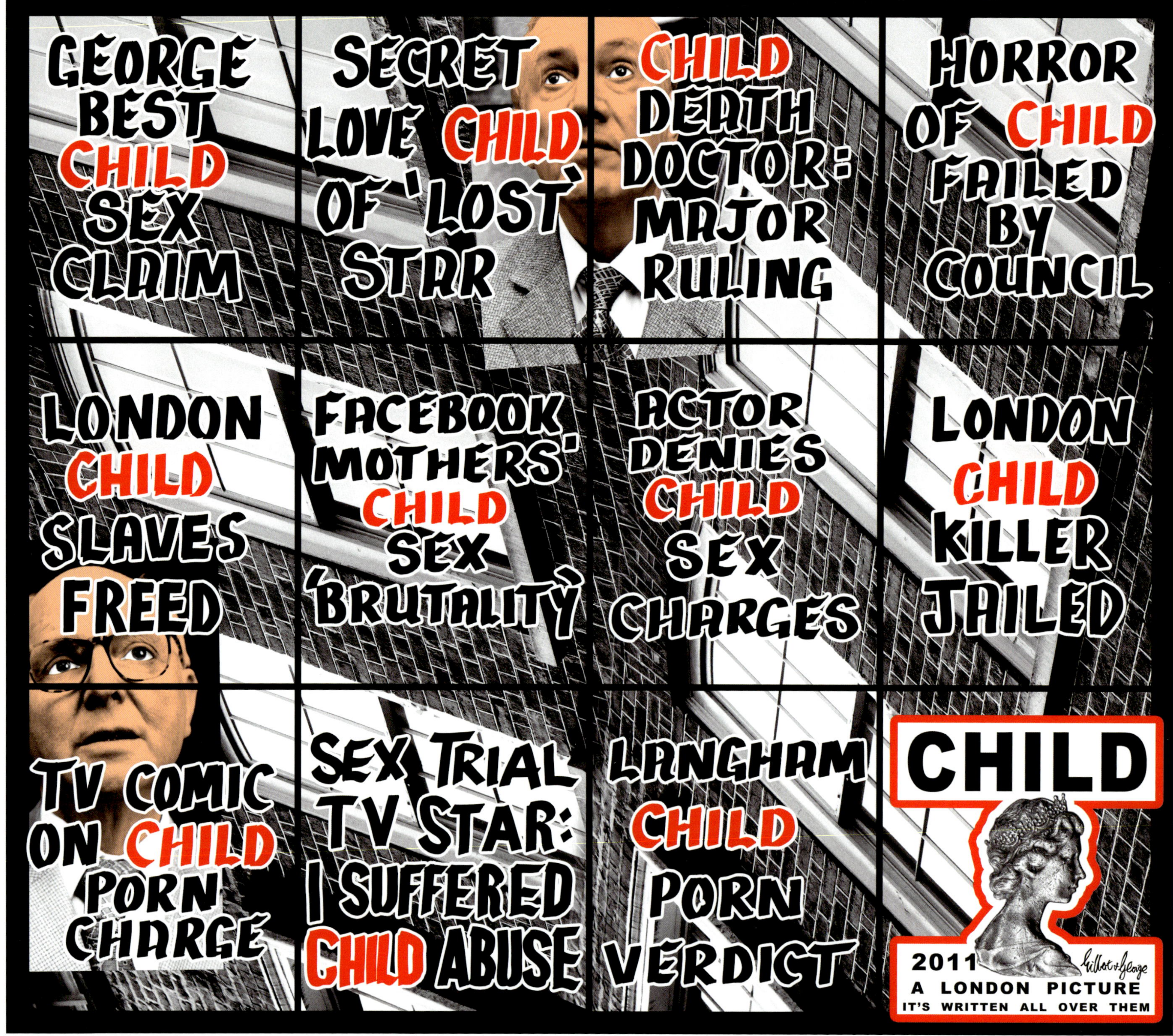

CHILD.   2011.   226 x 254 cm

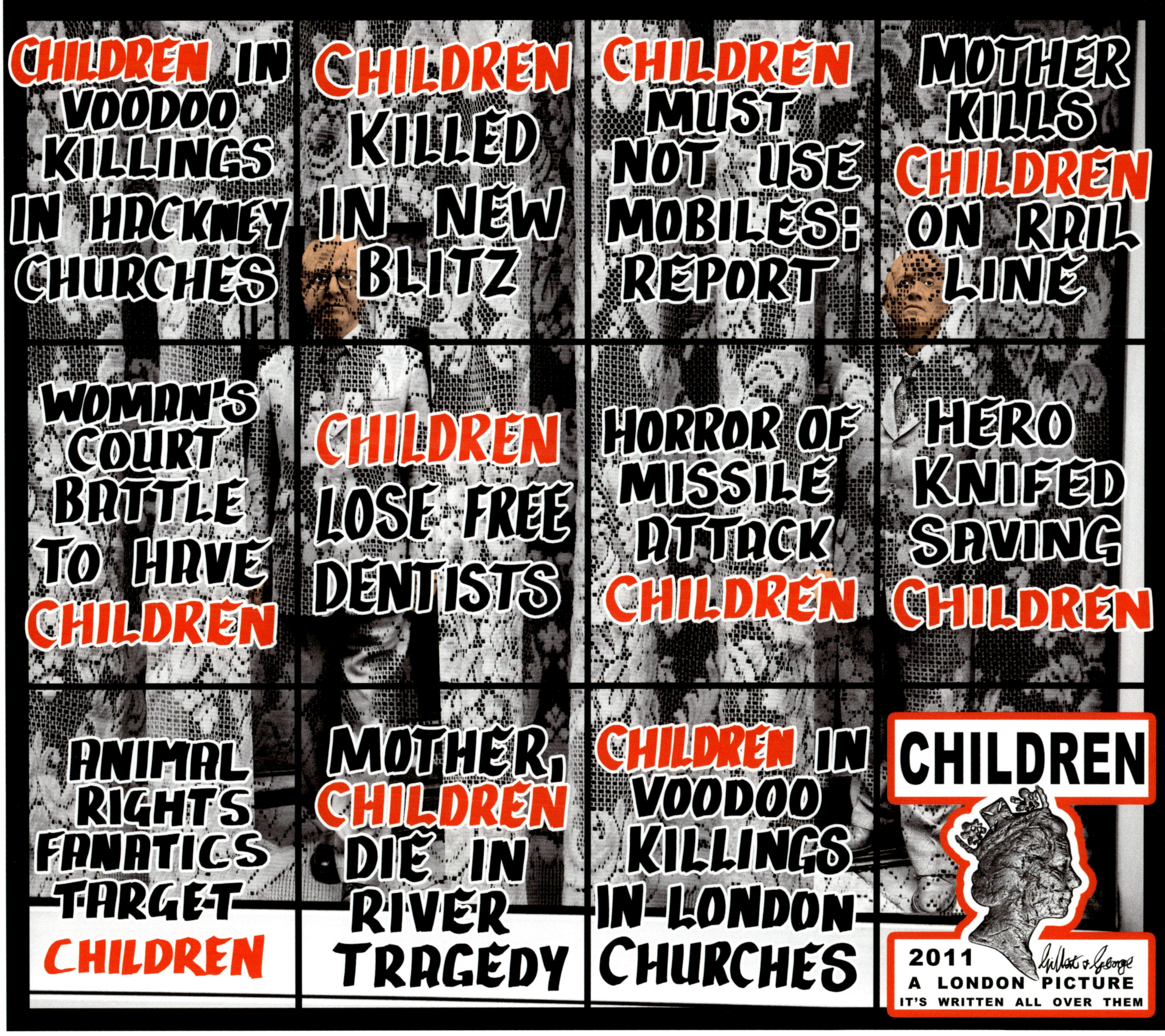

CHILDREN.   2011.   226 x 254 cm

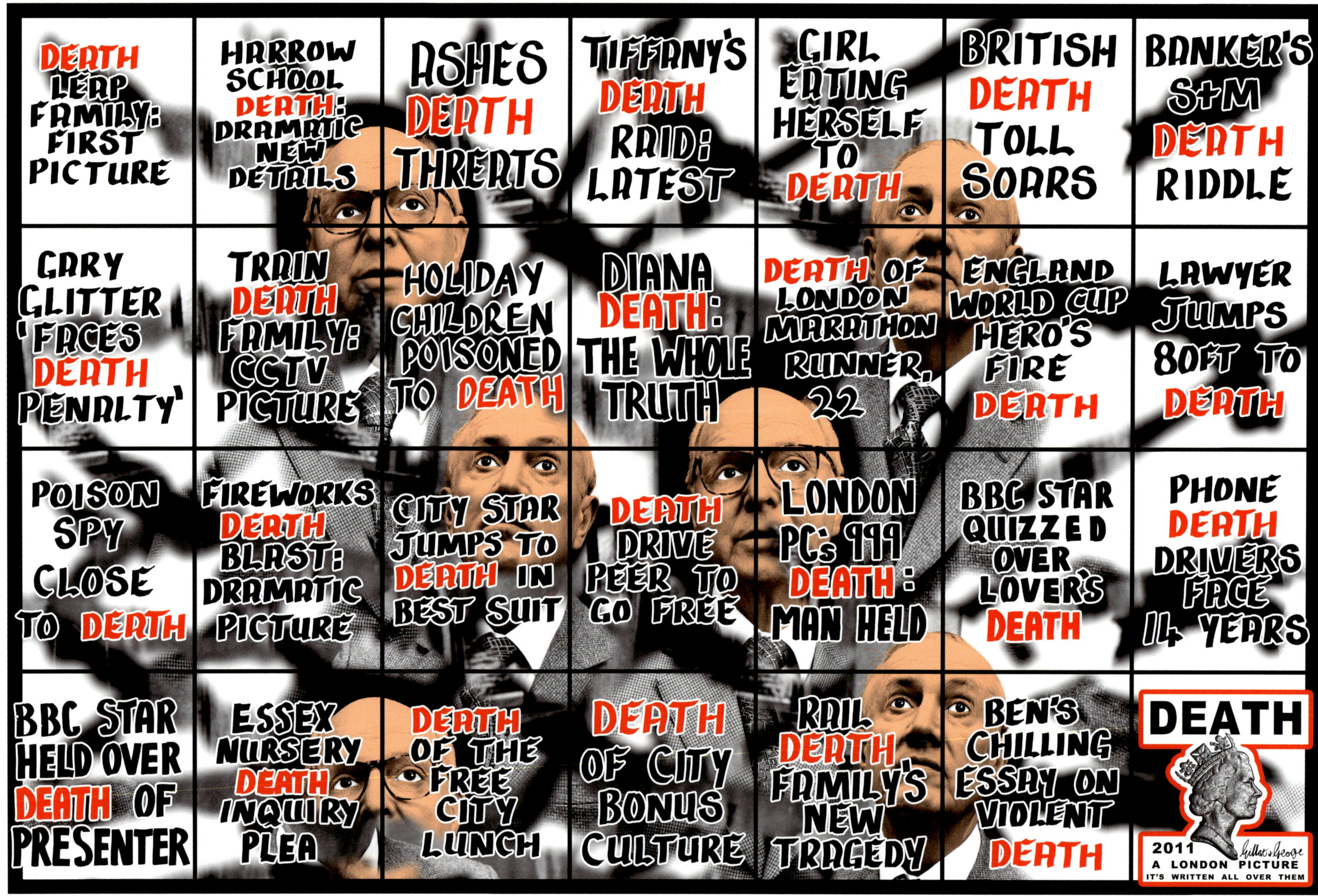

DEATH.   2011.   302 x 444 cm

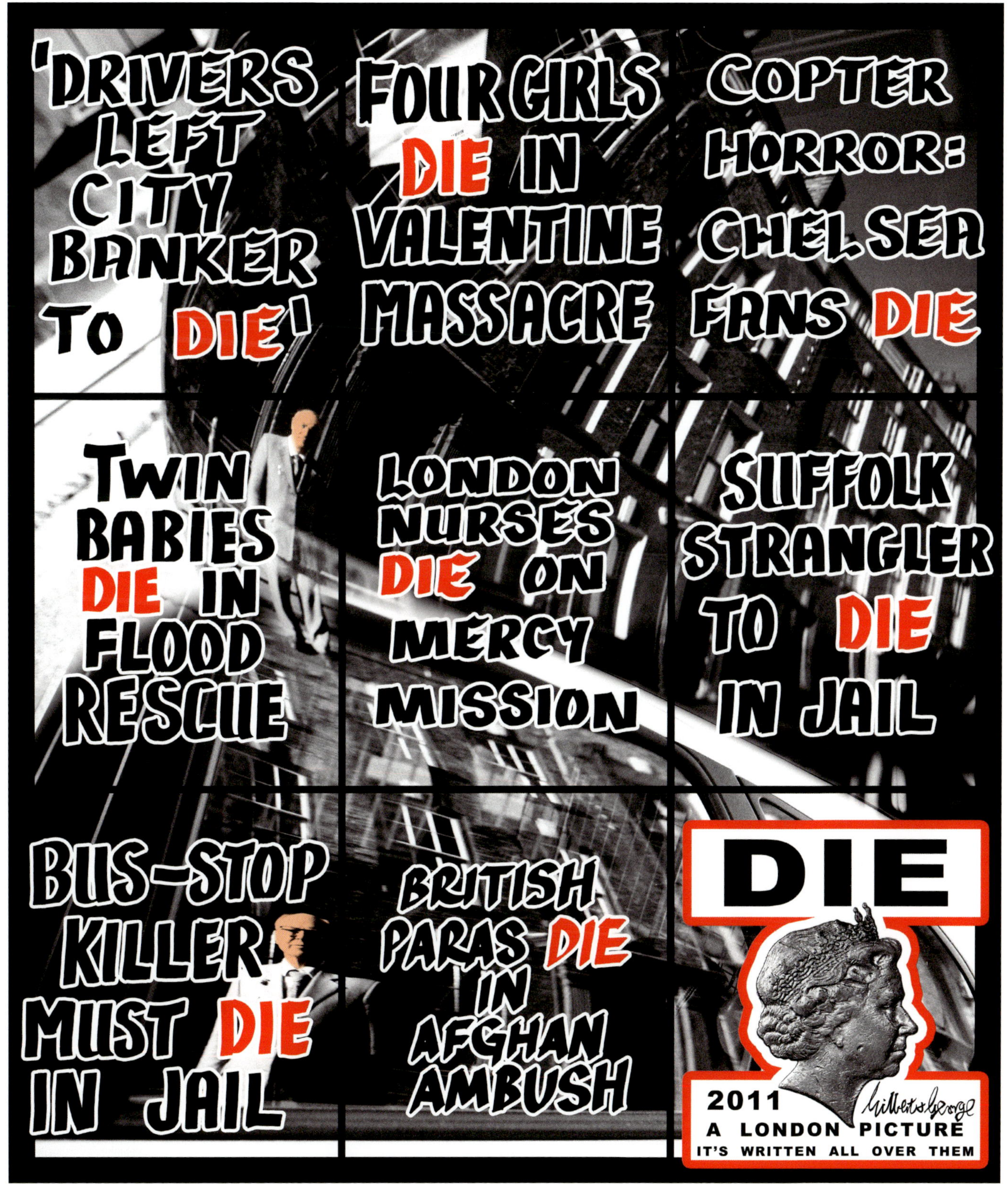

DIE.   2011.   226 x 190 cm

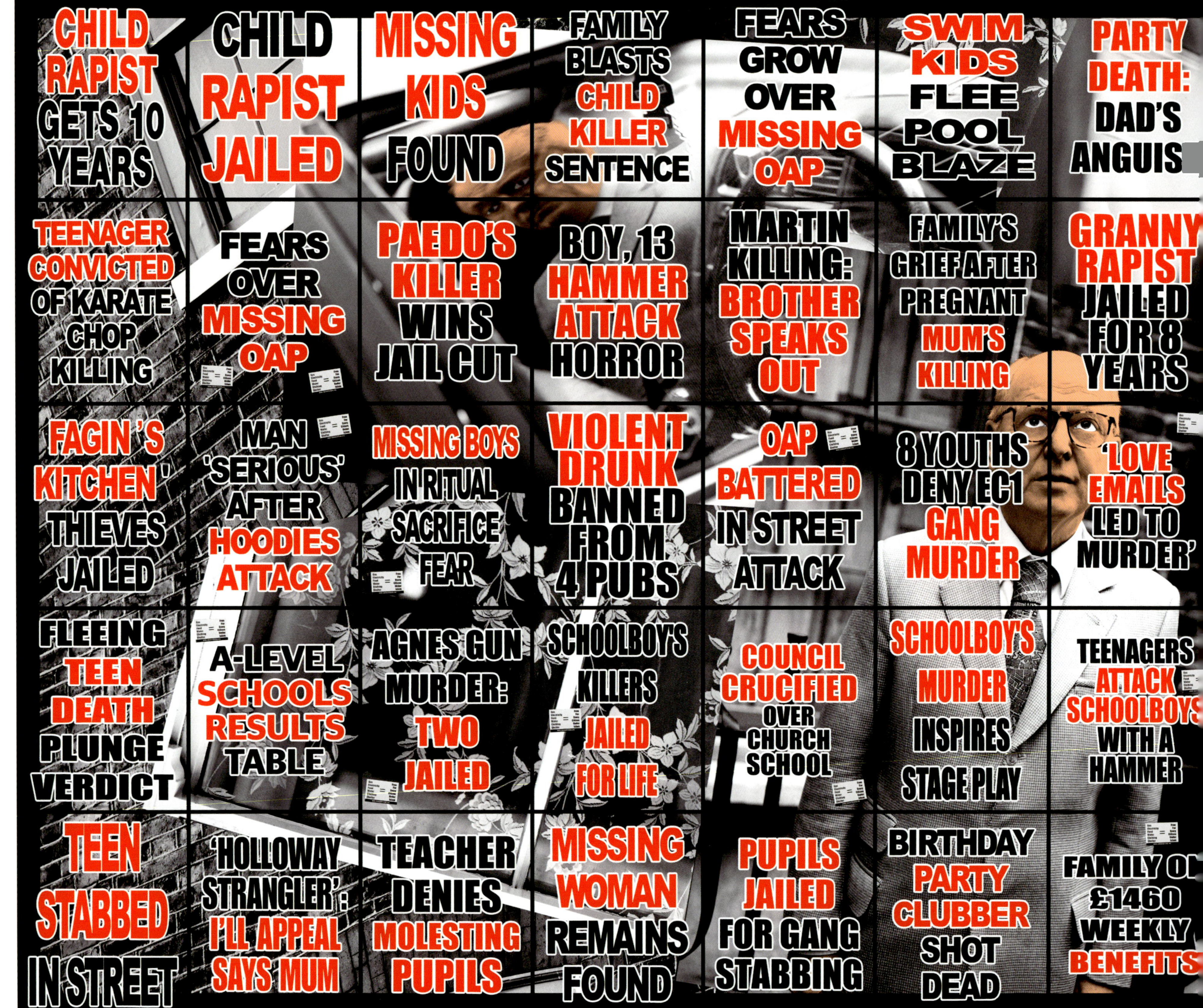

CHILD RAPIST GETS 10 YEARS
CHILD RAPIST JAILED
MISSING KIDS FOUND
FAMILY BLASTS CHILD KILLER SENTENCE
FEARS GROW OVER MISSING OAP
SWIM KIDS FLEE POOL BLAZE
PARTY DEATH: DAD'S ANGUIS
TEENAGER CONVICTED OF KARATE CHOP KILLING
FEARS OVER MISSING OAP
PAEDO'S KILLER WINS JAIL CUT
BOY, 13 HAMMER ATTACK HORROR
MARTIN KILLING: BROTHER SPEAKS OUT
FAMILY'S GRIEF AFTER PREGNANT MUM'S KILLING
GRANNY RAPIST JAILED FOR 8 YEARS
FAGIN'S KITCHEN THIEVES JAILED
MAN 'SERIOUS' AFTER HOODIES ATTACK
MISSING BOYS IN RITUAL SACRIFICE FEAR
VIOLENT DRUNK BANNED FROM 4 PUBS
OAP BATTERED IN STREET ATTACK
8 YOUTHS DENY EC1 GANG MURDER
'LOVE EMAILS LED TO MURDER'
FLEEING TEEN DEATH PLUNGE VERDICT
A-LEVEL SCHOOLS RESULTS TABLE
AGNES GUN MURDER: TWO JAILED
SCHOOLBOY'S KILLERS JAILED FOR LIFE
COUNCIL CRUCIFIED OVER CHURCH SCHOOL
SCHOOLBOY'S MURDER INSPIRES STAGE PLAY
TEENAGERS ATTACK SCHOOLBOYS WITH A HAMMER
TEEN STABBED IN STREET
'HOLLOWAY STRANGLER': I'LL APPEAL SAYS MUM
TEACHER DENIES MOLESTING PUPILS
MISSING WOMAN REMAINS FOUND
PUPILS JAILED FOR GANG STABBING
BIRTHDAY PARTY CLUBBER SHOT DEAD
FAMILY ON £1460 WEEKLY BENEFITS

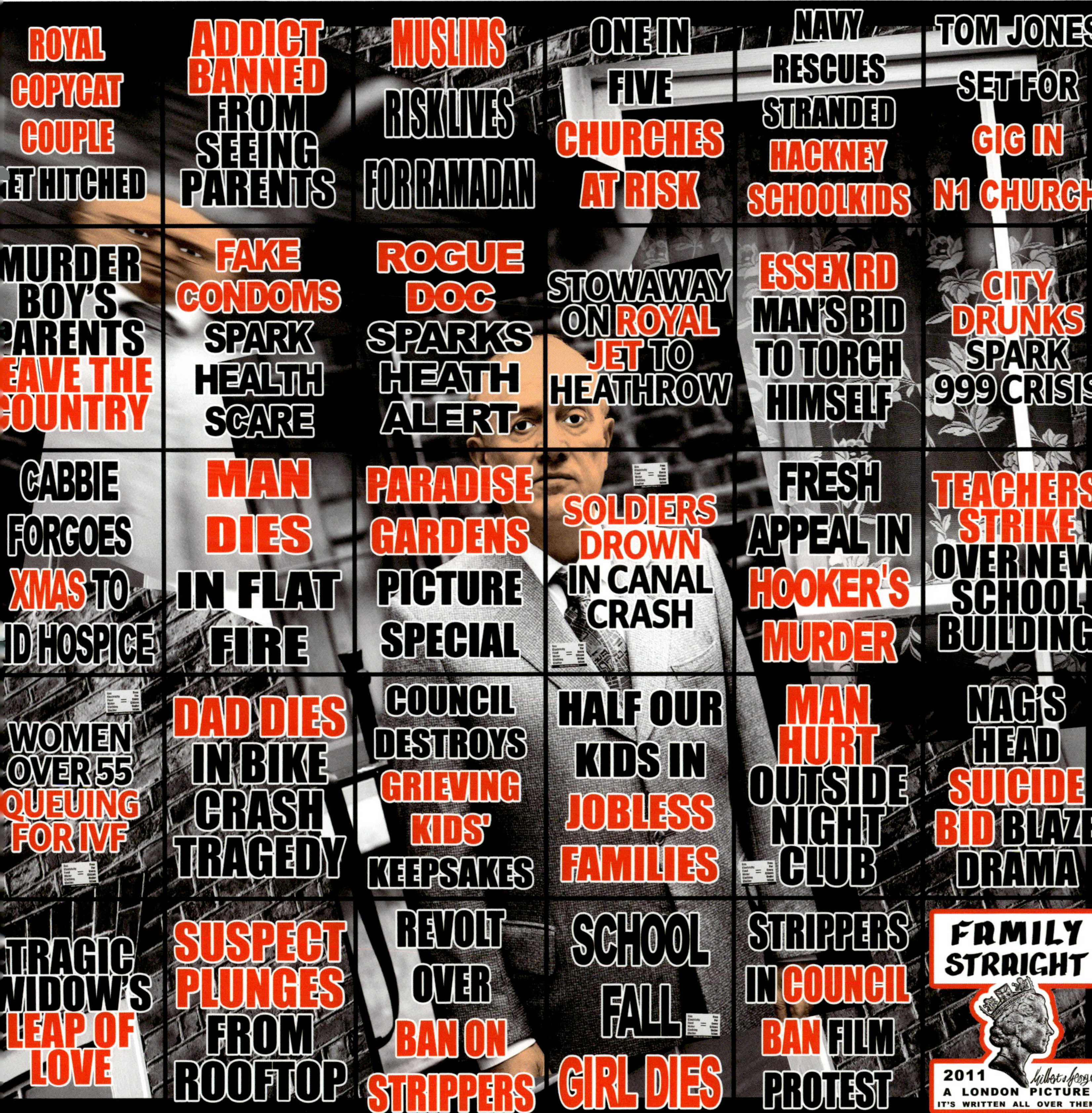

FAMILY STRAIGHT

2011

377 x 825 cm

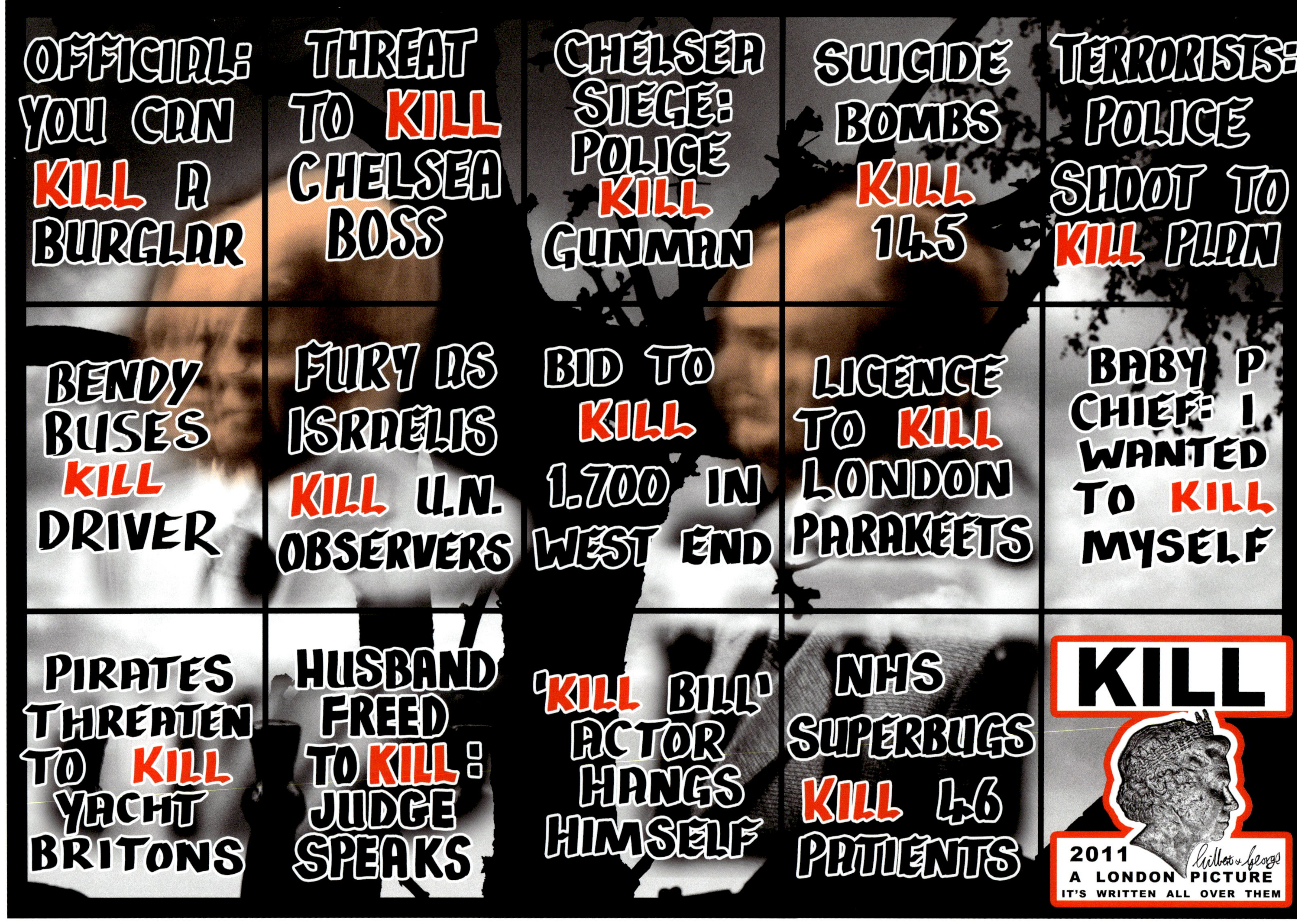

KILL. 2011. 226 x 317 cm

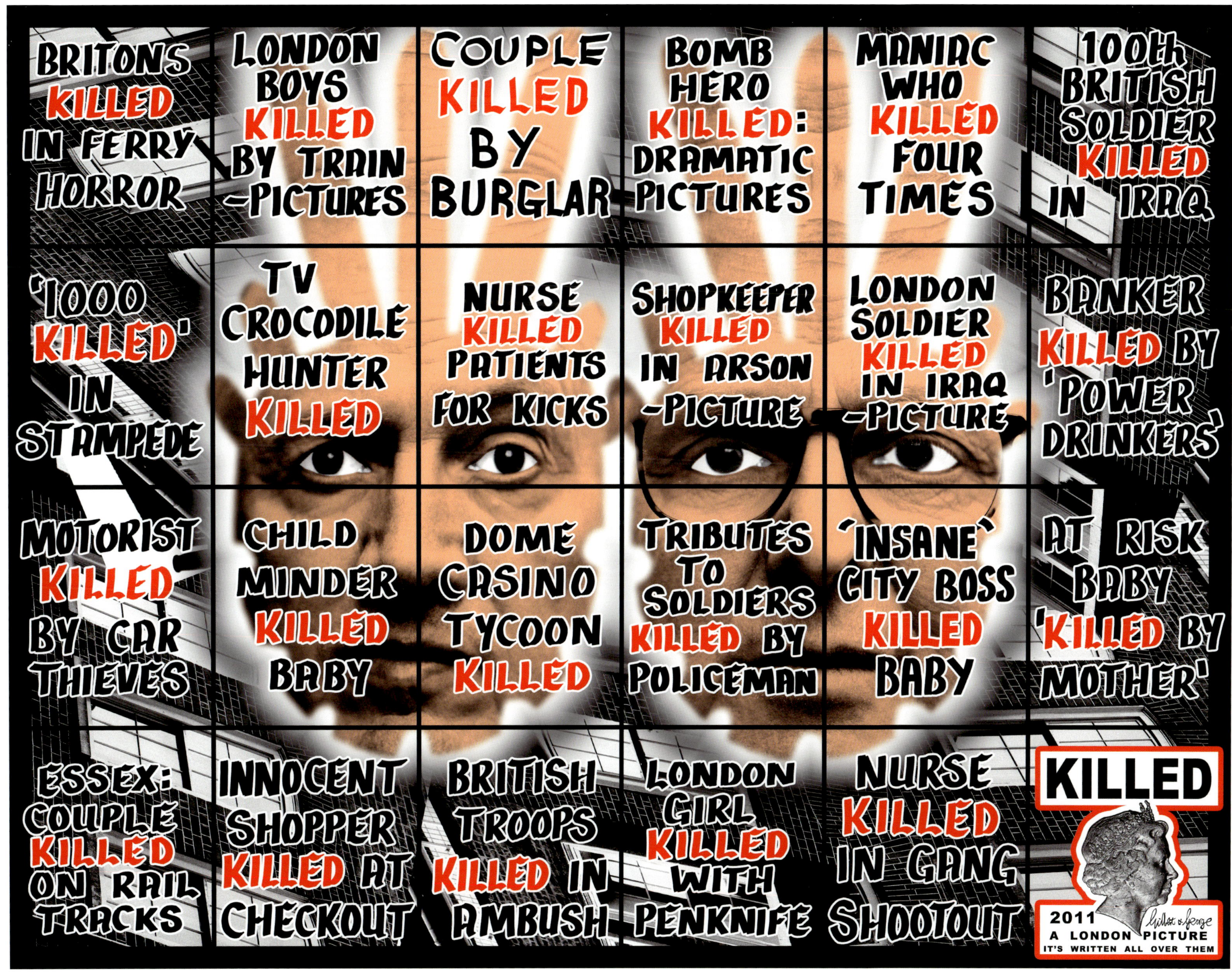

KILLED.   2011.   302 x 381 cm

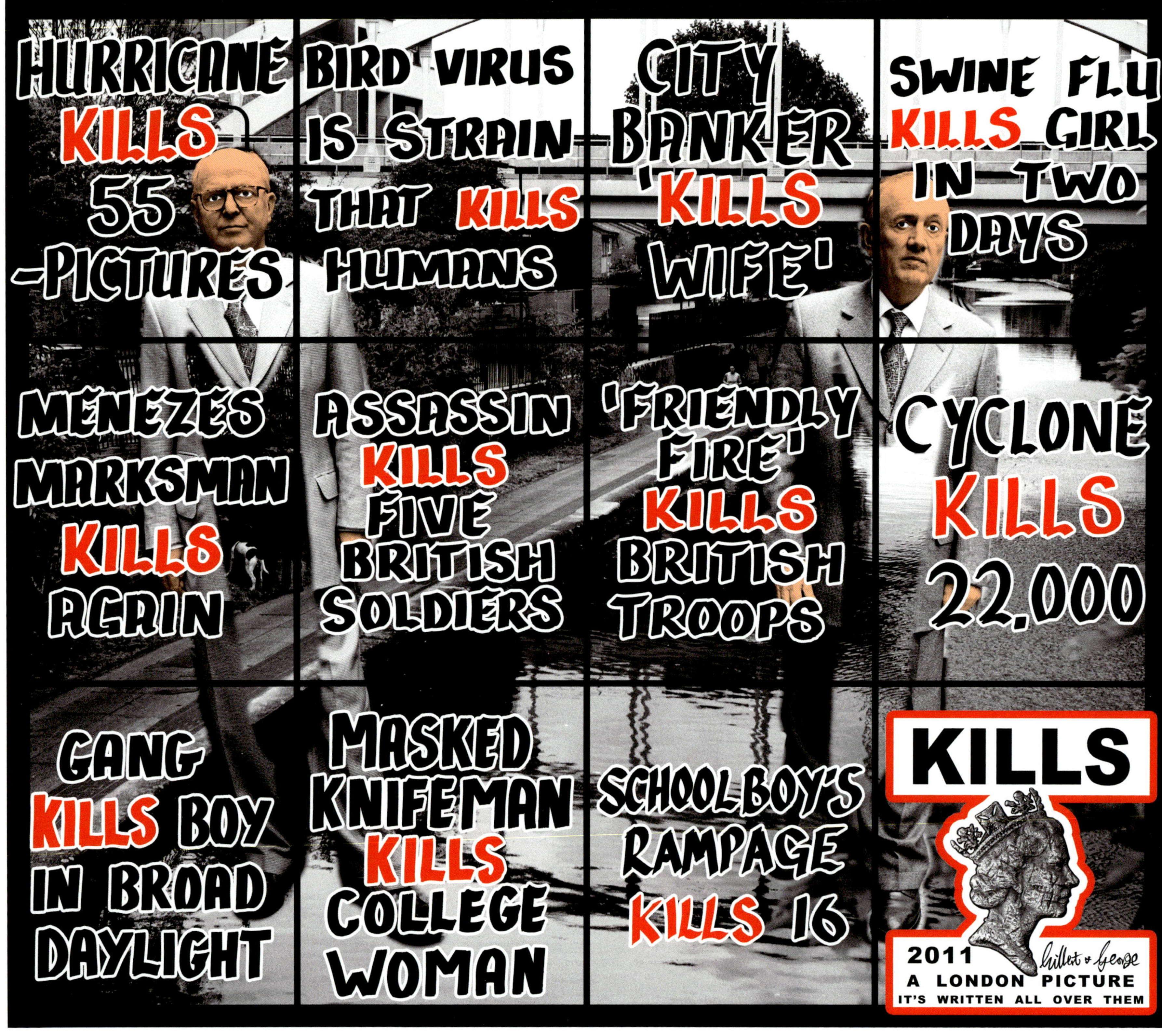

KILLS.   2011.   226 x 254 cm

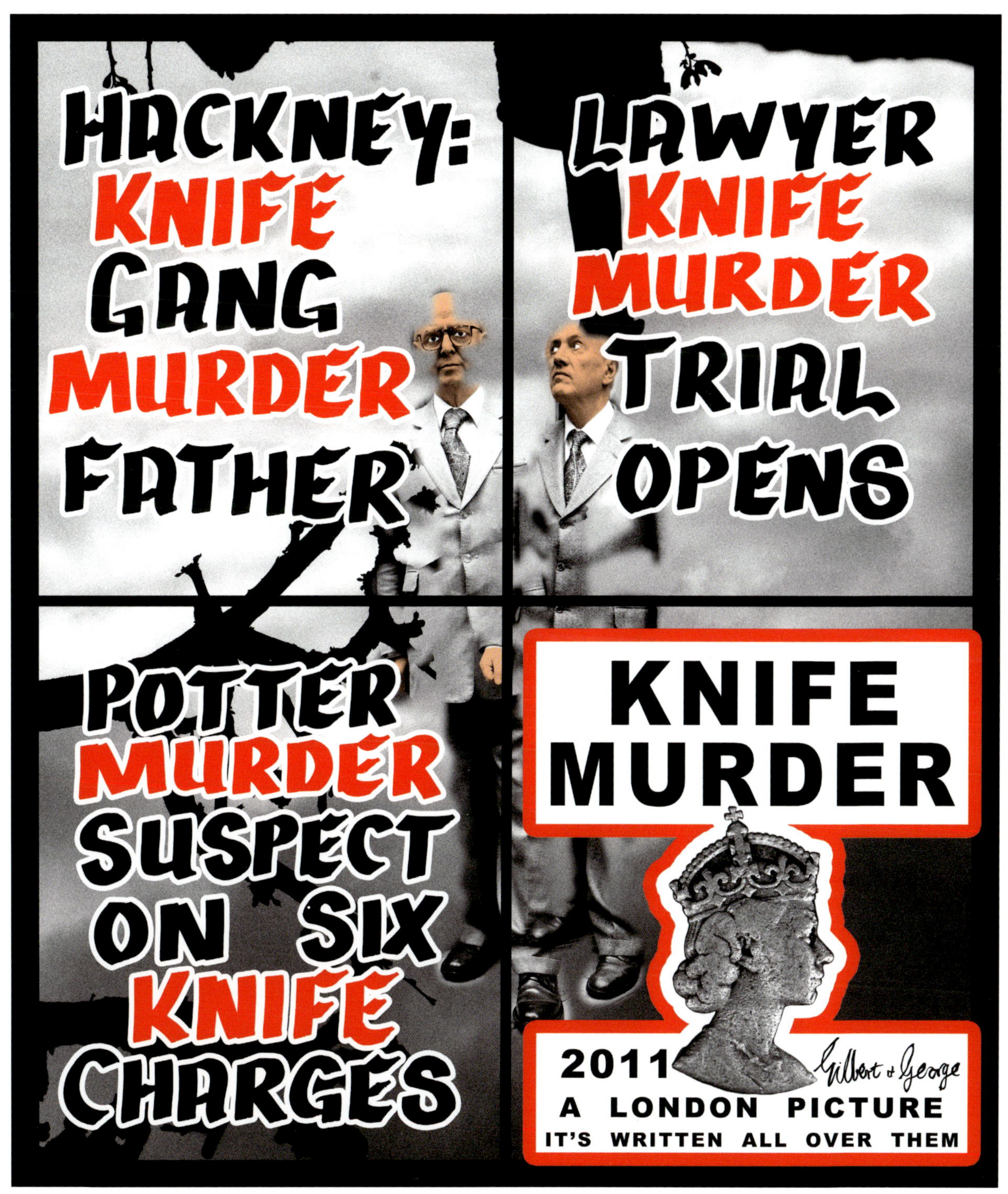

KNIFE MURDER.   2011.   151 x 127 cm

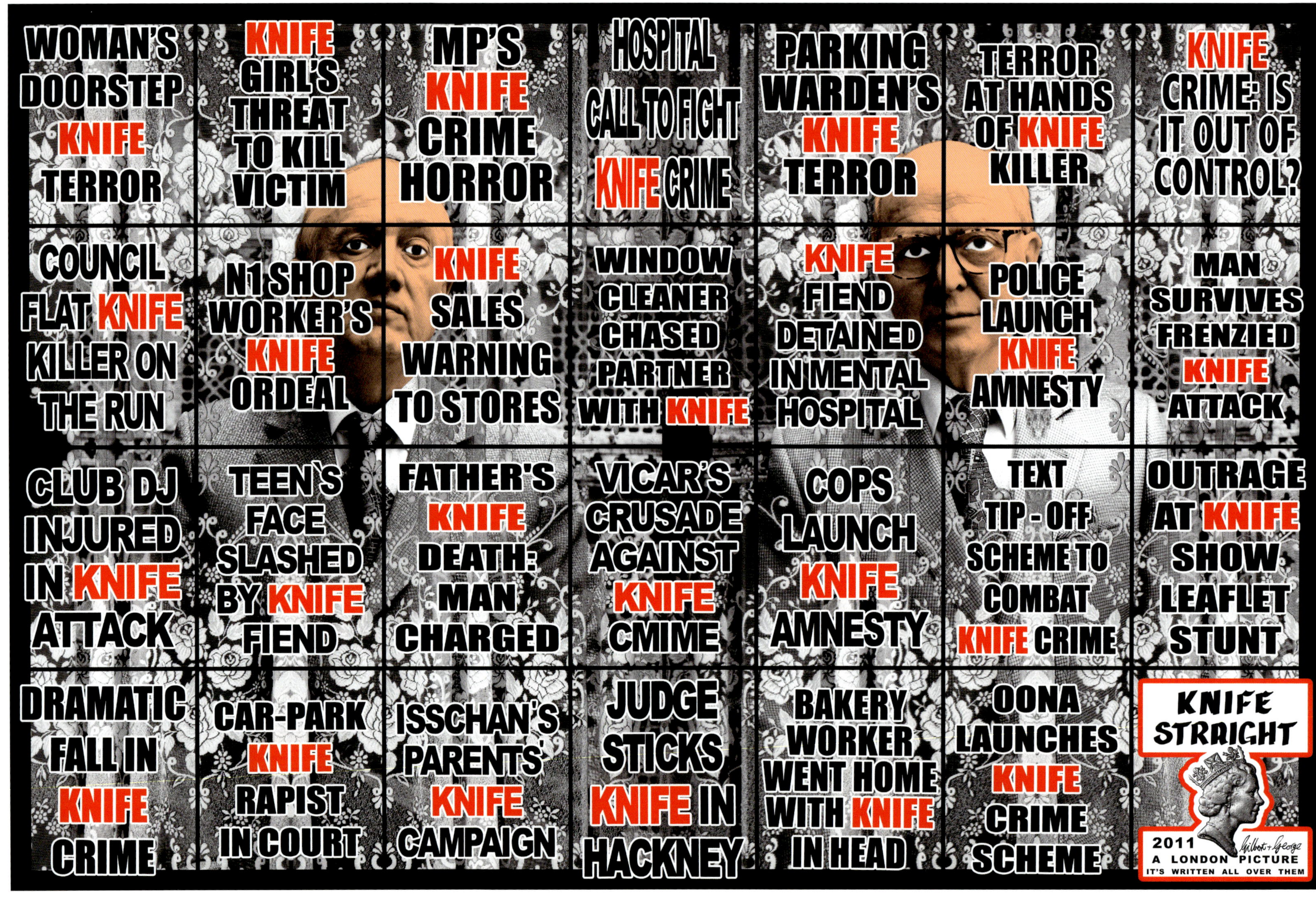

KNIFE STRAIGHT. 2011. 302 x 444 cm

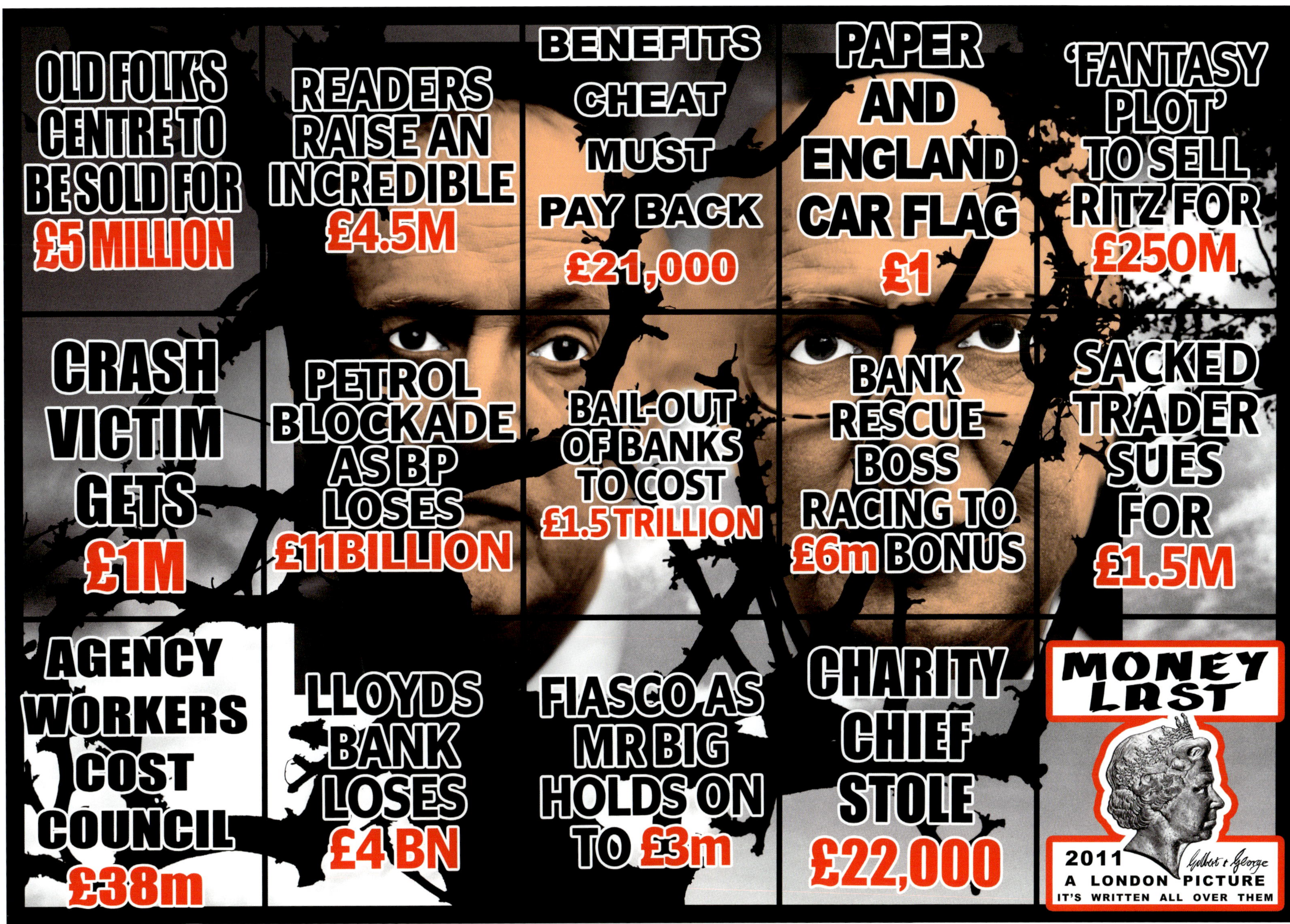

MONEY LAST.   2011.   226 x 317 cm

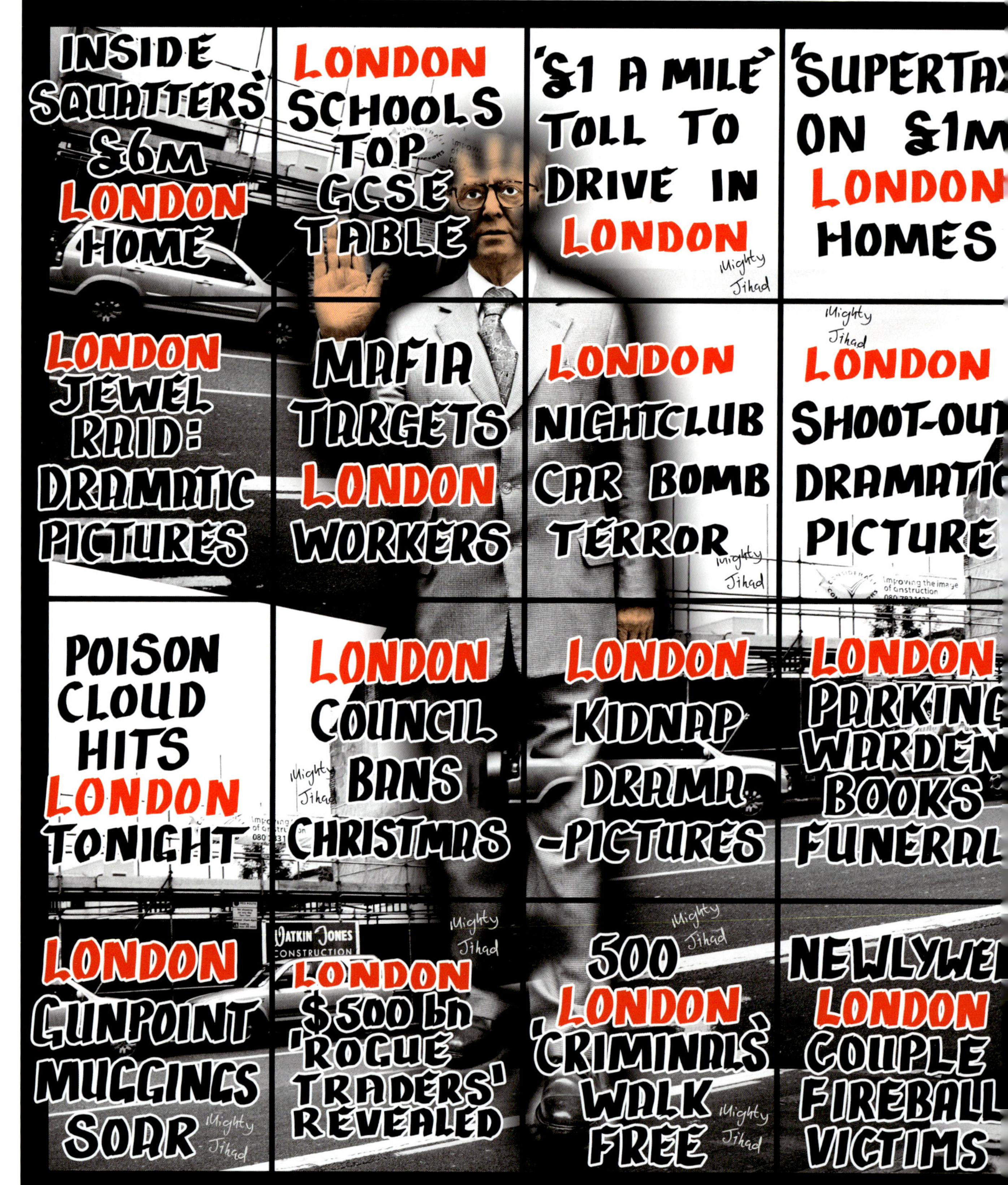

LONDON. 2011. 302 x 508 cm

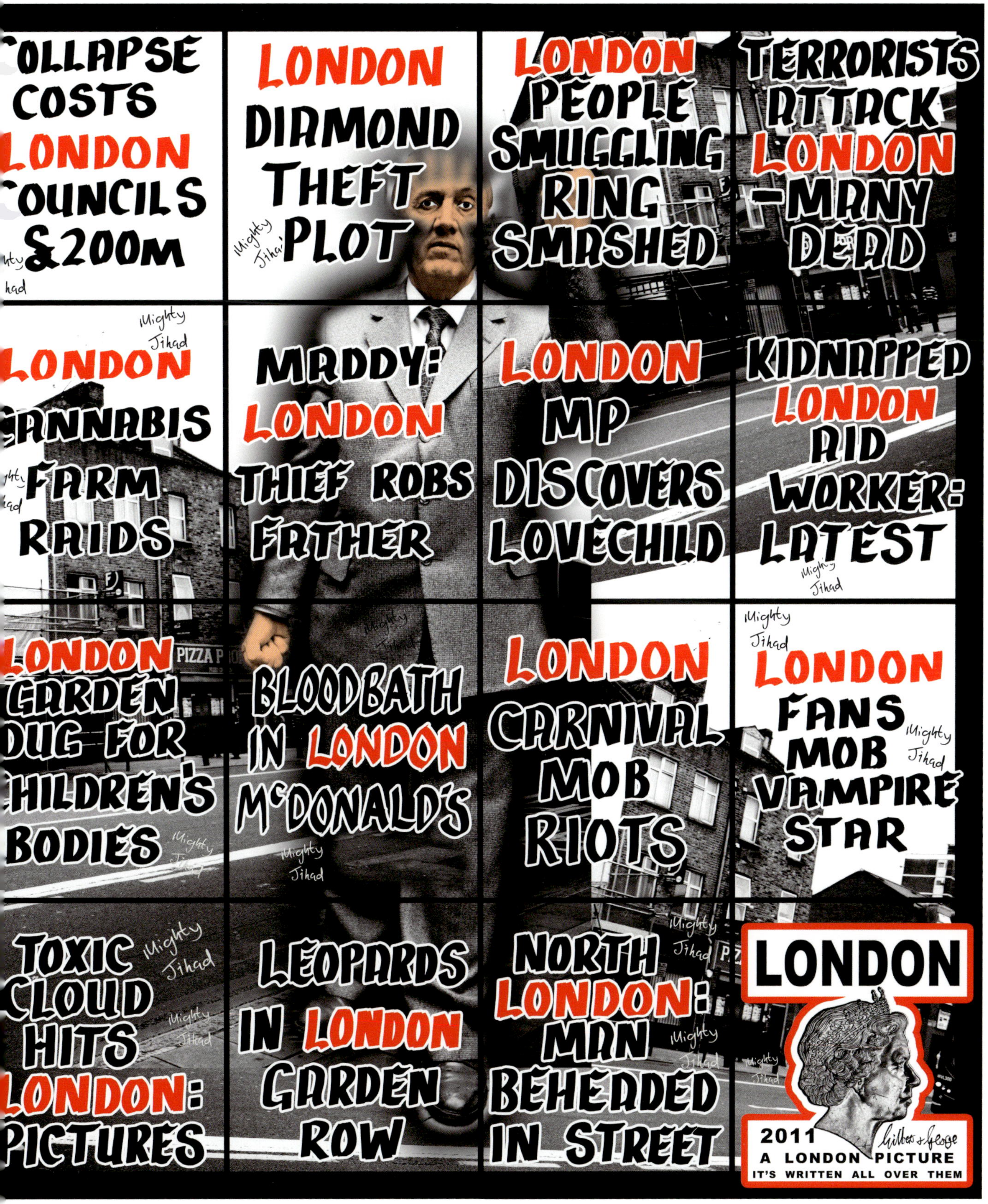

COLLAPSE COSTS LONDON COUNCILS £200M

LONDON DIAMOND THEFT PLOT

LONDON PEOPLE SMUGGLING RING SMASHED

TERRORISTS ATTACK LONDON — MANY DEAD

LONDON CANNABIS FARM RAIDS

MADDY: LONDON THIEF ROBS FATHER

LONDON MP DISCOVERS LOVECHILD

KIDNAPPED LONDON AID WORKER: LATEST

LONDON GARDEN DUG FOR CHILDREN'S BODIES

BLOODBATH IN LONDON McDONALD'S

LONDON CARNIVAL MOB RIOTS

LONDON FANS MOB VAMPIRE STAR

TOXIC CLOUD HITS LONDON: PICTURES

LEOPARDS IN LONDON GARDEN ROW

NORTH LONDON: MAN BEHEADED IN STREET

LONDON

2011
A LONDON PICTURE
IT'S WRITTEN ALL OVER THEM

Mighty Jihad

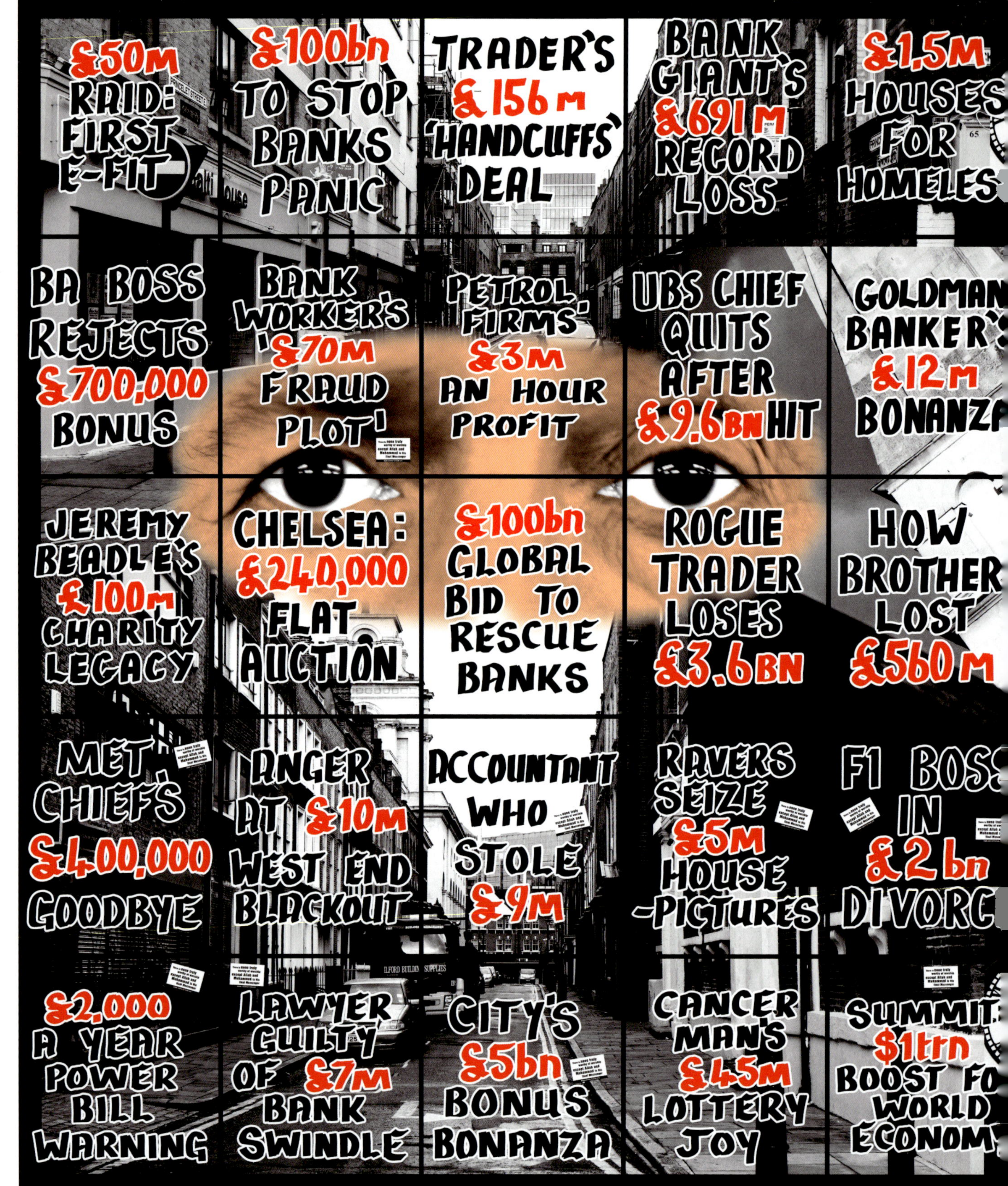

MONEY. 2011. 377 x 698 cm

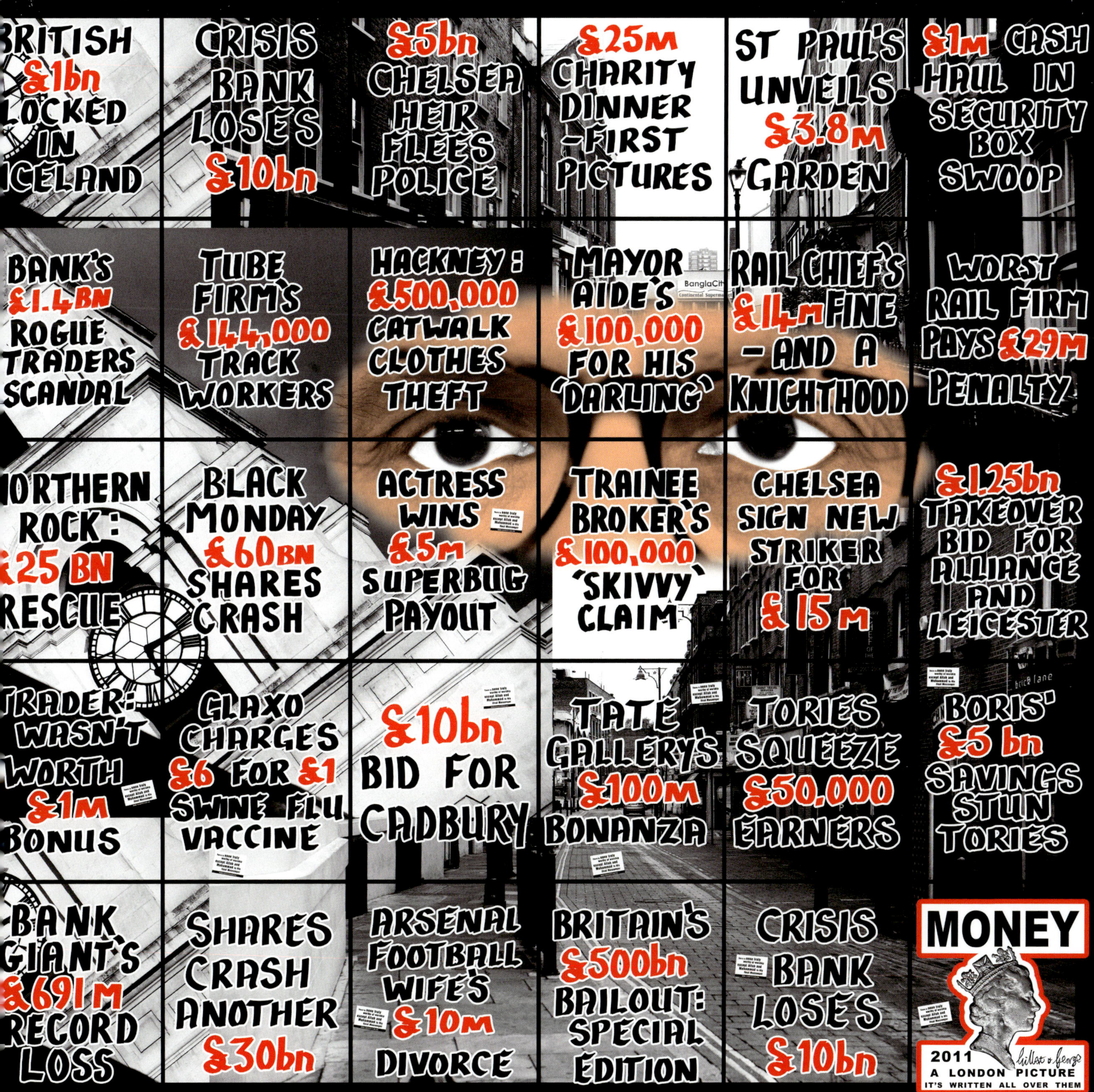

BRITISH £1bn LOCKED IN ICELAND
CRISIS BANK LOSES £10bn
£5bn CHELSEA HEIR FLEES POLICE
£25M CHARITY DINNER - FIRST PICTURES
ST PAUL'S UNVEILS £3.8M GARDEN
£1M CASH HAUL IN SECURITY BOX SWOOP
BANK'S £1.4BN ROGUE TRADERS SCANDAL
TUBE FIRM'S £144,000 TRACK WORKERS
HACKNEY: £500,000 CATWALK CLOTHES THEFT
MAYOR AIDE'S £100,000 FOR HIS 'DARLING'
RAIL CHIEF'S £14M FINE - AND A KNIGHTHOOD
WORST RAIL FIRM PAYS £29M PENALTY
NORTHERN ROCK: £25 BN RESCUE
BLACK MONDAY £60BN SHARES CRASH
ACTRESS WINS £5M SUPERBUG PAYOUT
TRAINEE BROKER'S £100,000 'SKIVVY' CLAIM
CHELSEA SIGN NEW STRIKER FOR £15M
£1.25bn TAKEOVER BID FOR ALLIANCE AND LEICESTER
TRADER: WASN'T WORTH £1M BONUS
GLAXO CHARGES £6 FOR £1 SWINE FLU VACCINE
£10bn BID FOR CADBURY
TATE GALLERY'S £100M BONANZA
TORIES SQUEEZE £50,000 EARNERS
BORIS' £5 bn SAVINGS STUN TORIES
BANK GIANT'S £691M RECORD LOSS
SHARES CRASH ANOTHER £30bn
ARSENAL FOOTBALL WIFE'S £10M DIVORCE
BRITAIN'S £500bn BAILOUT: SPECIAL EDITION
CRISIS BANK LOSES £10bn
MONEY
2011
A LONDON PICTURE
IT'S WRITTEN ALL OVER THEM

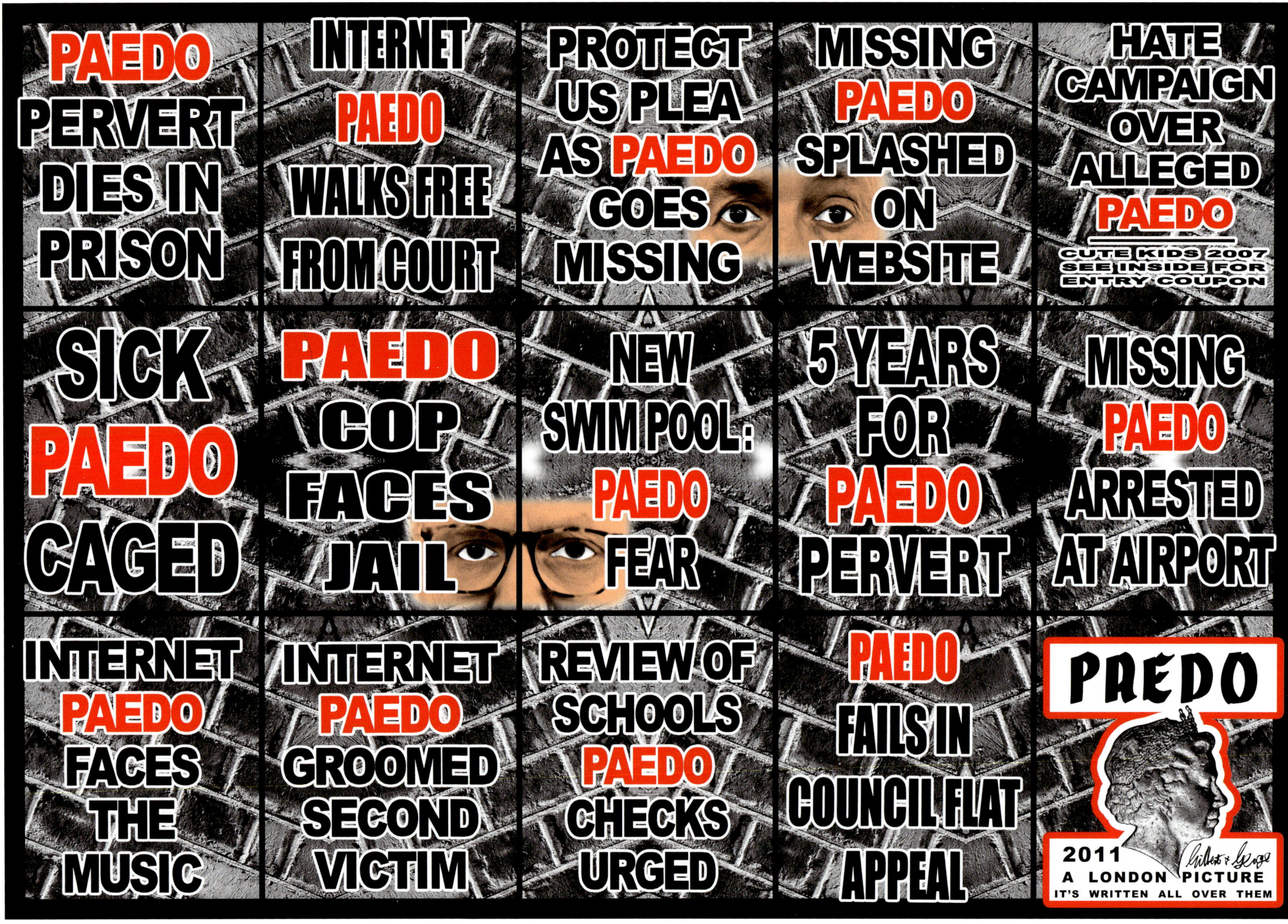

PAEDO.   2011.   226 x 317 cm

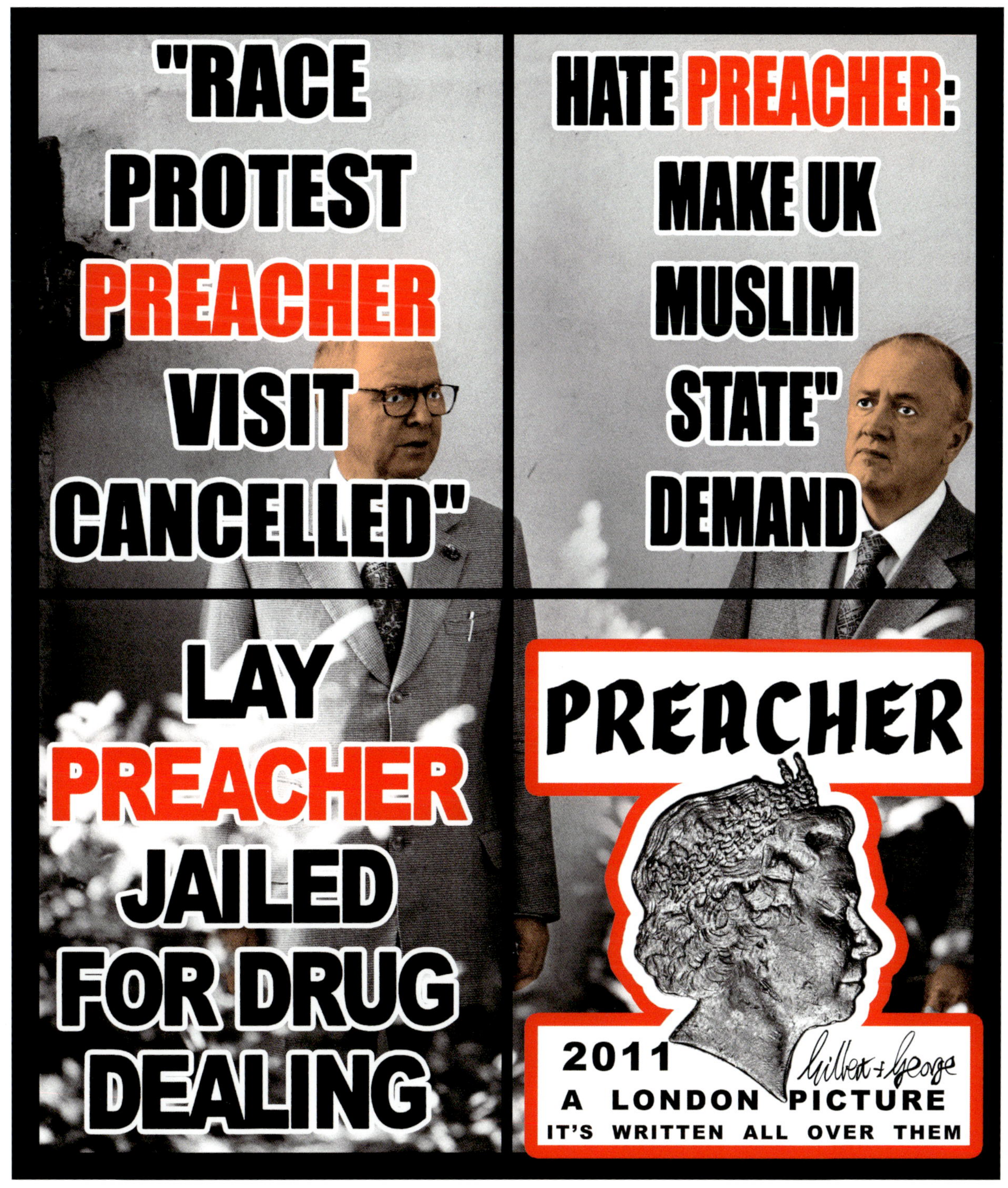

PREACHER.   2011.   151 x 127 cm

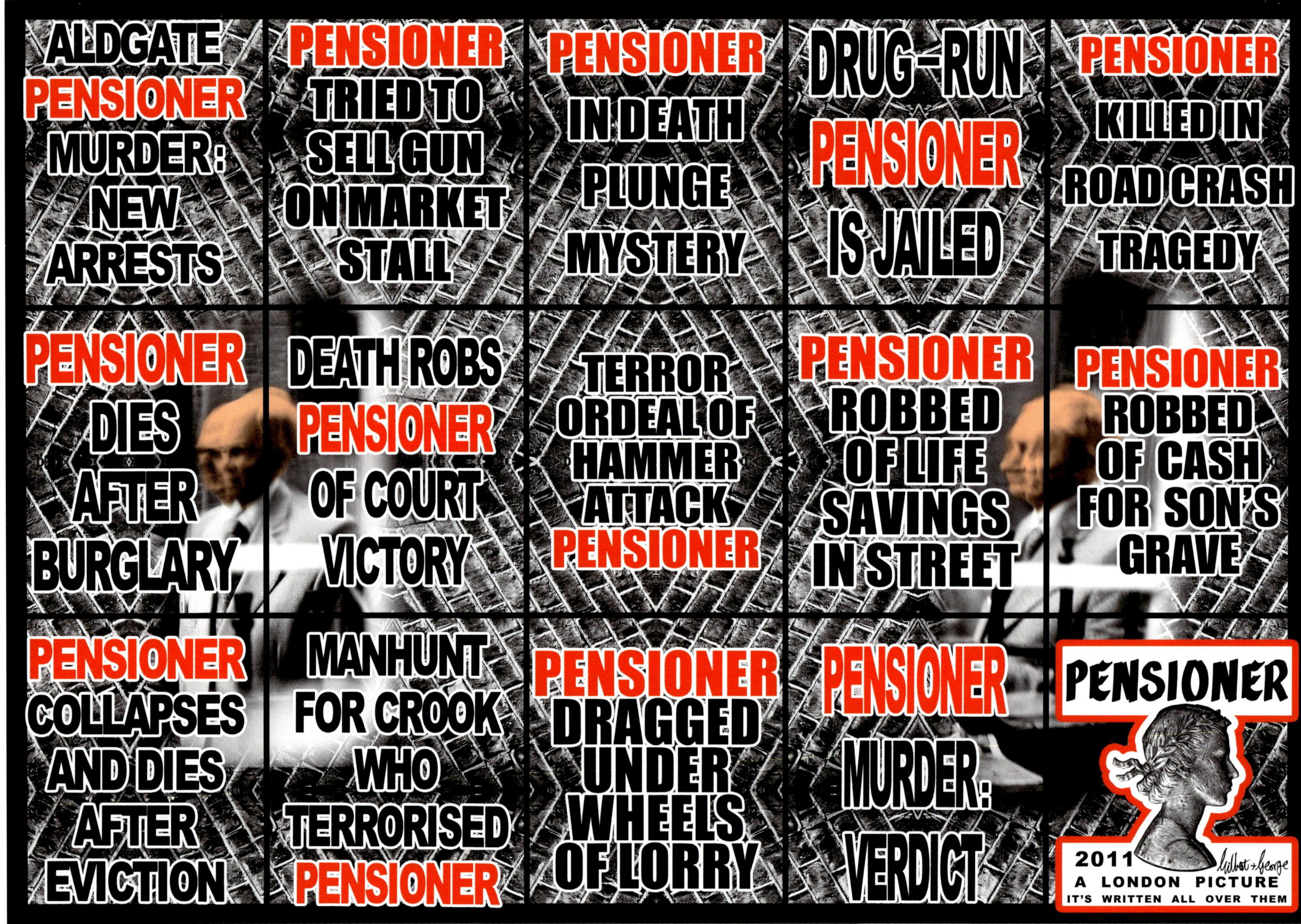

PENSIONER.   2011.   226 x 317 cm

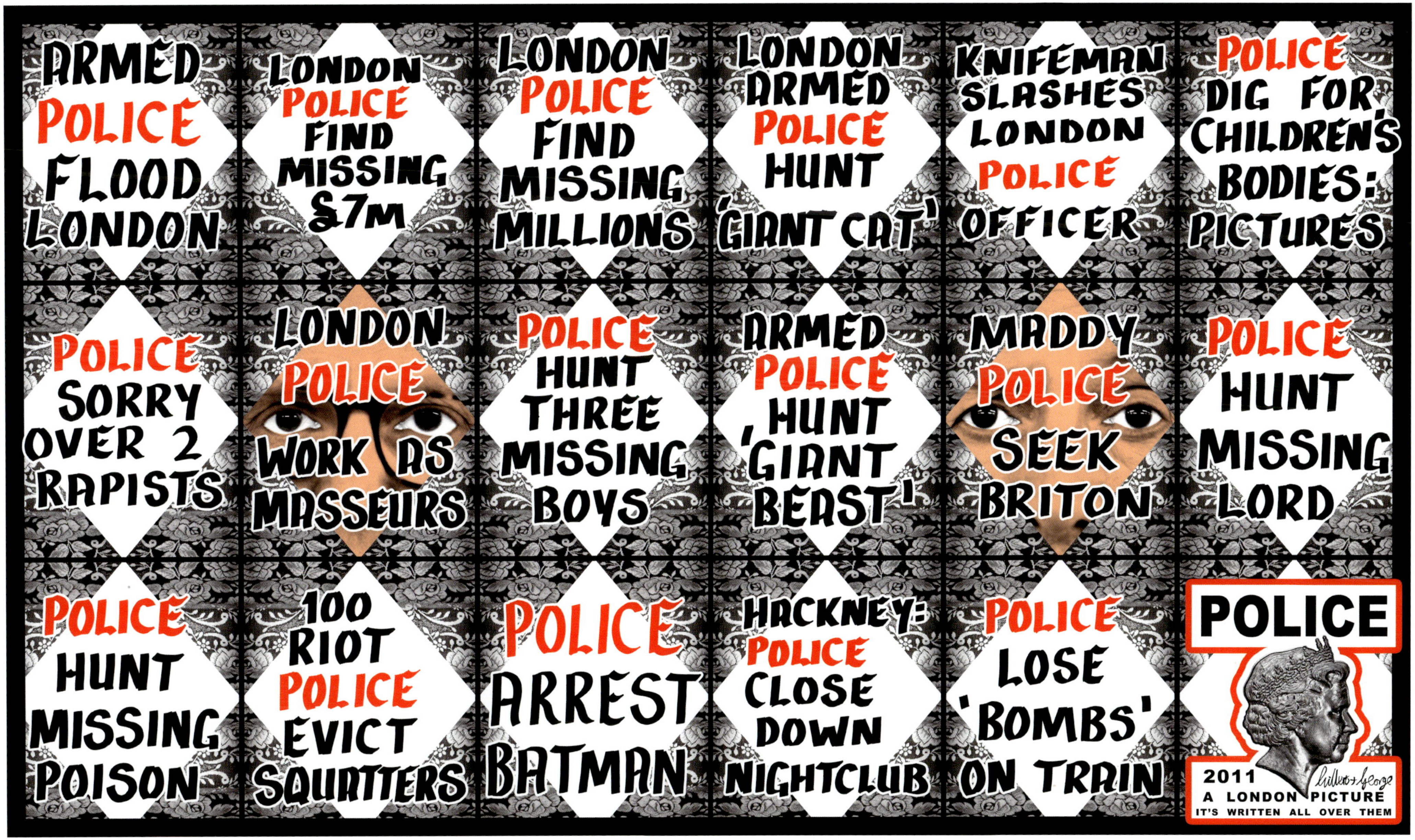

POLICE. 2011. 226 x 381 cm

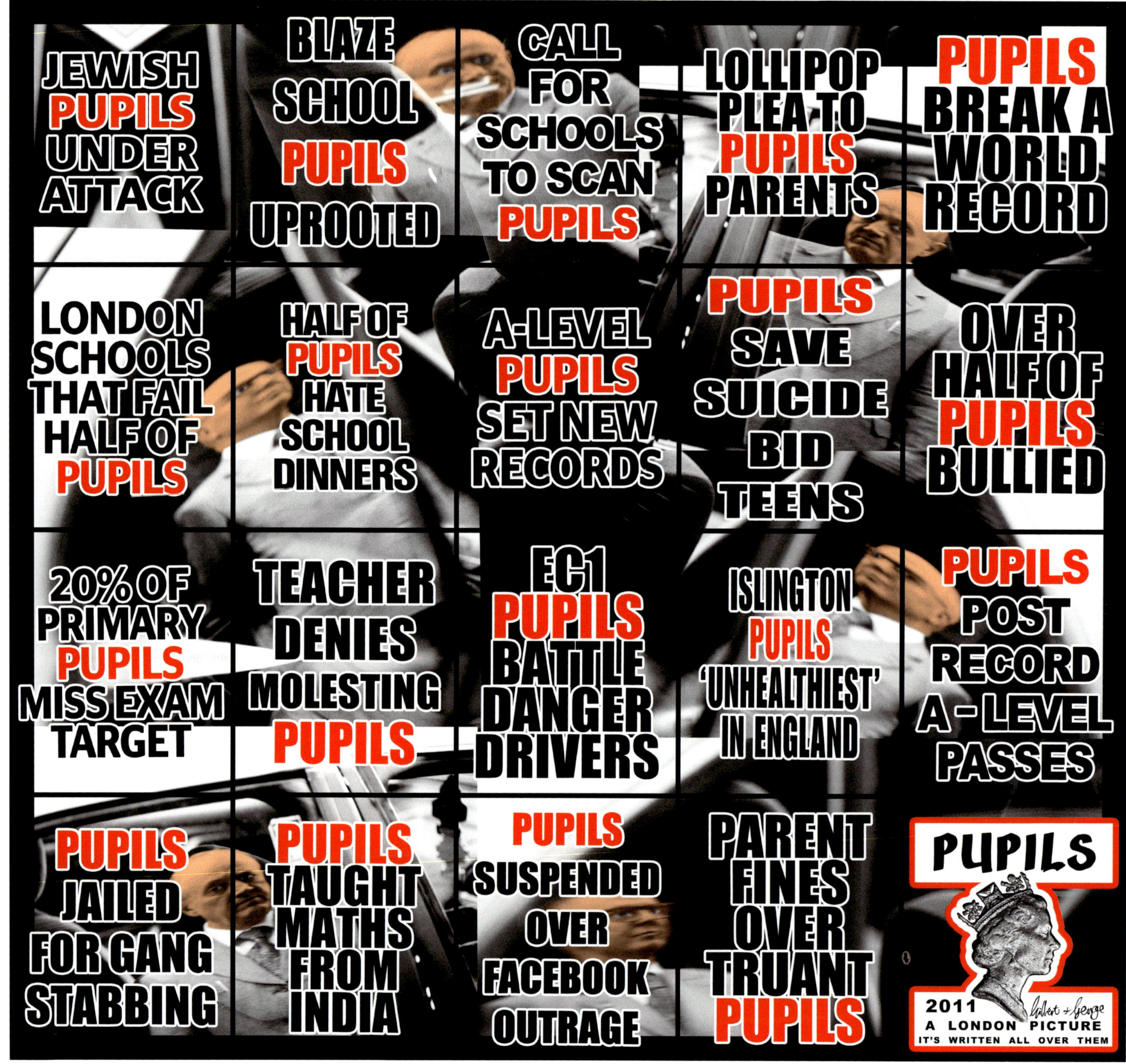

PUPILS.   2011.   302 x 317 cm

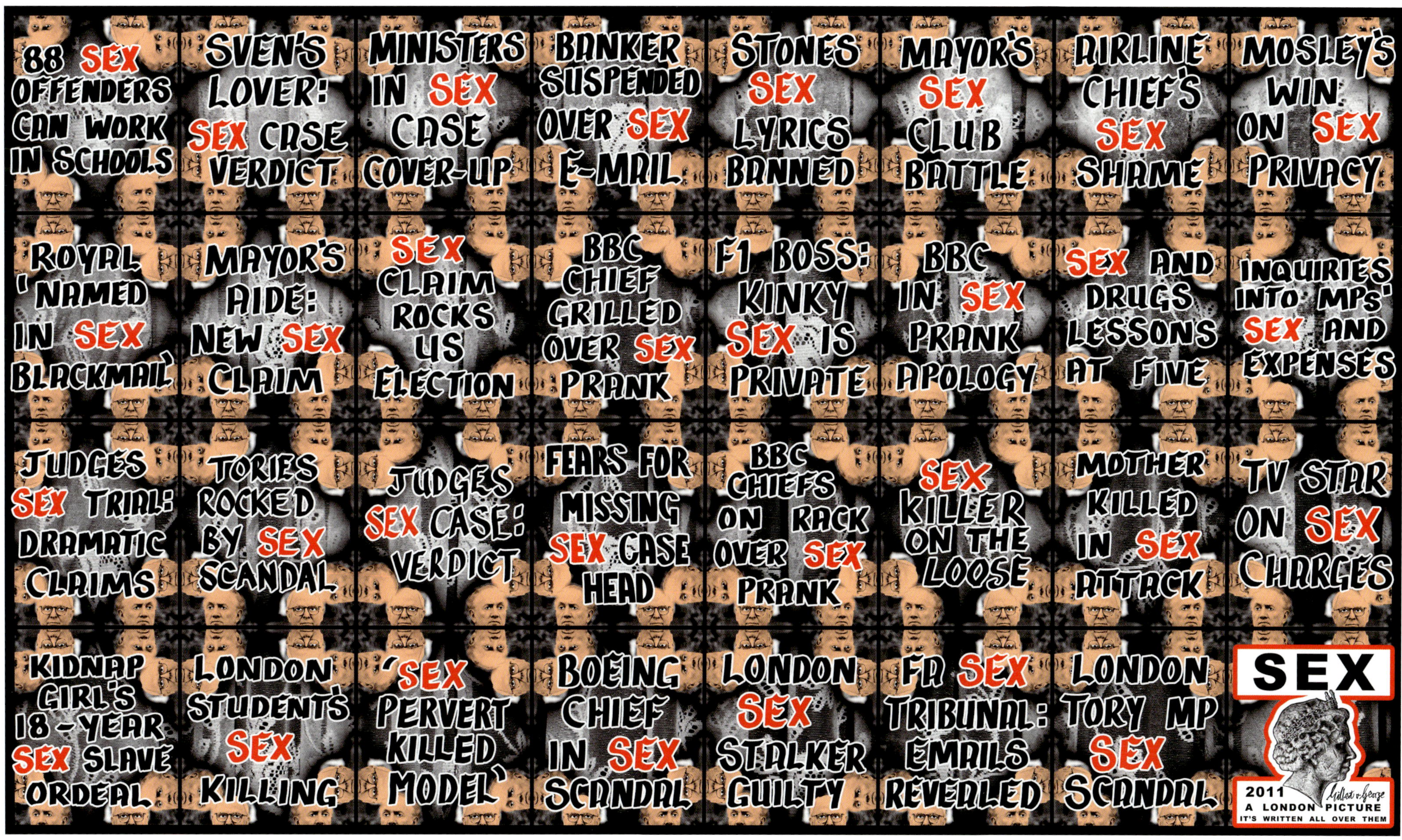

SEX.   2011.   302 x 508 cm

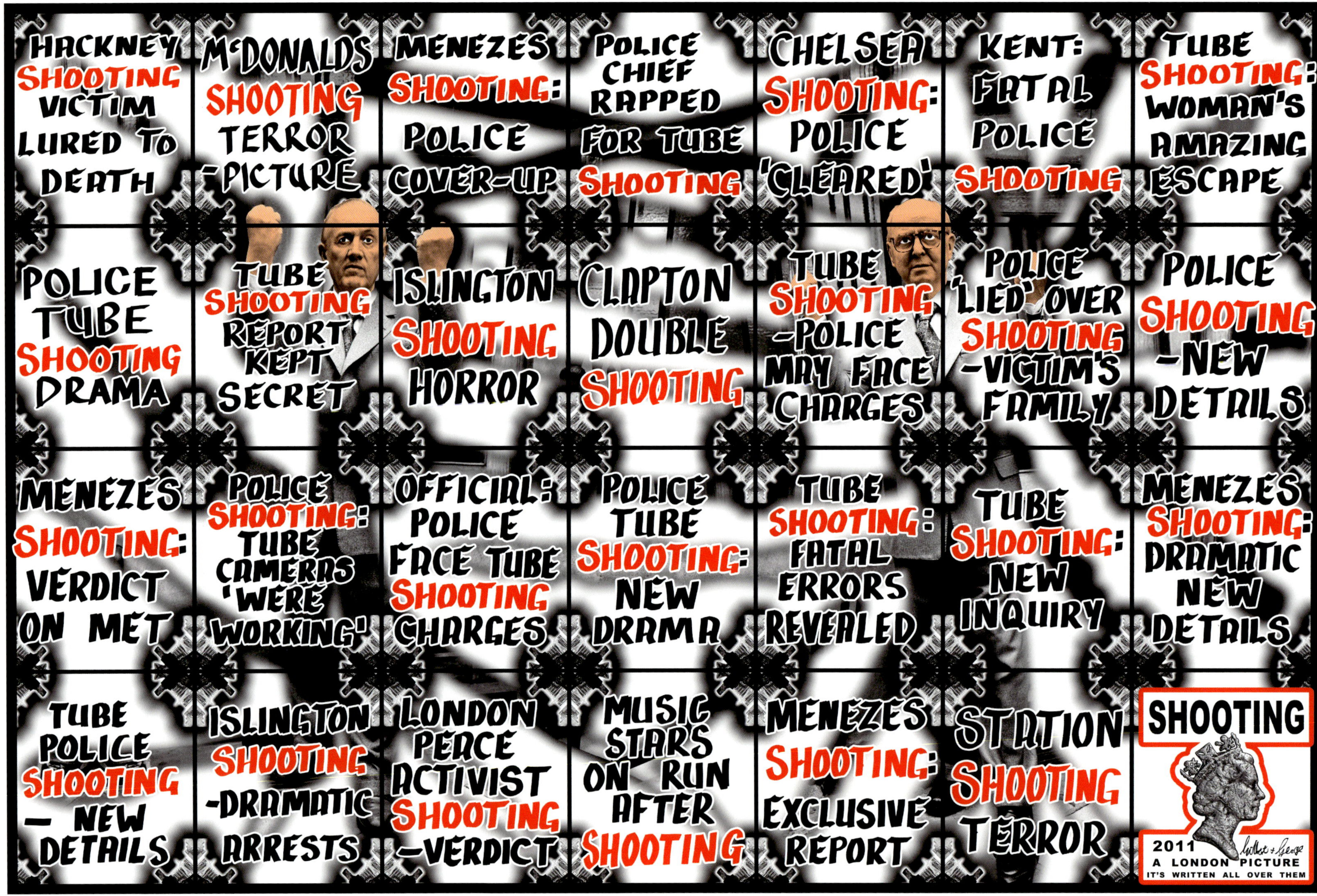

SHOOTING.   2011.   302 x 444 cm

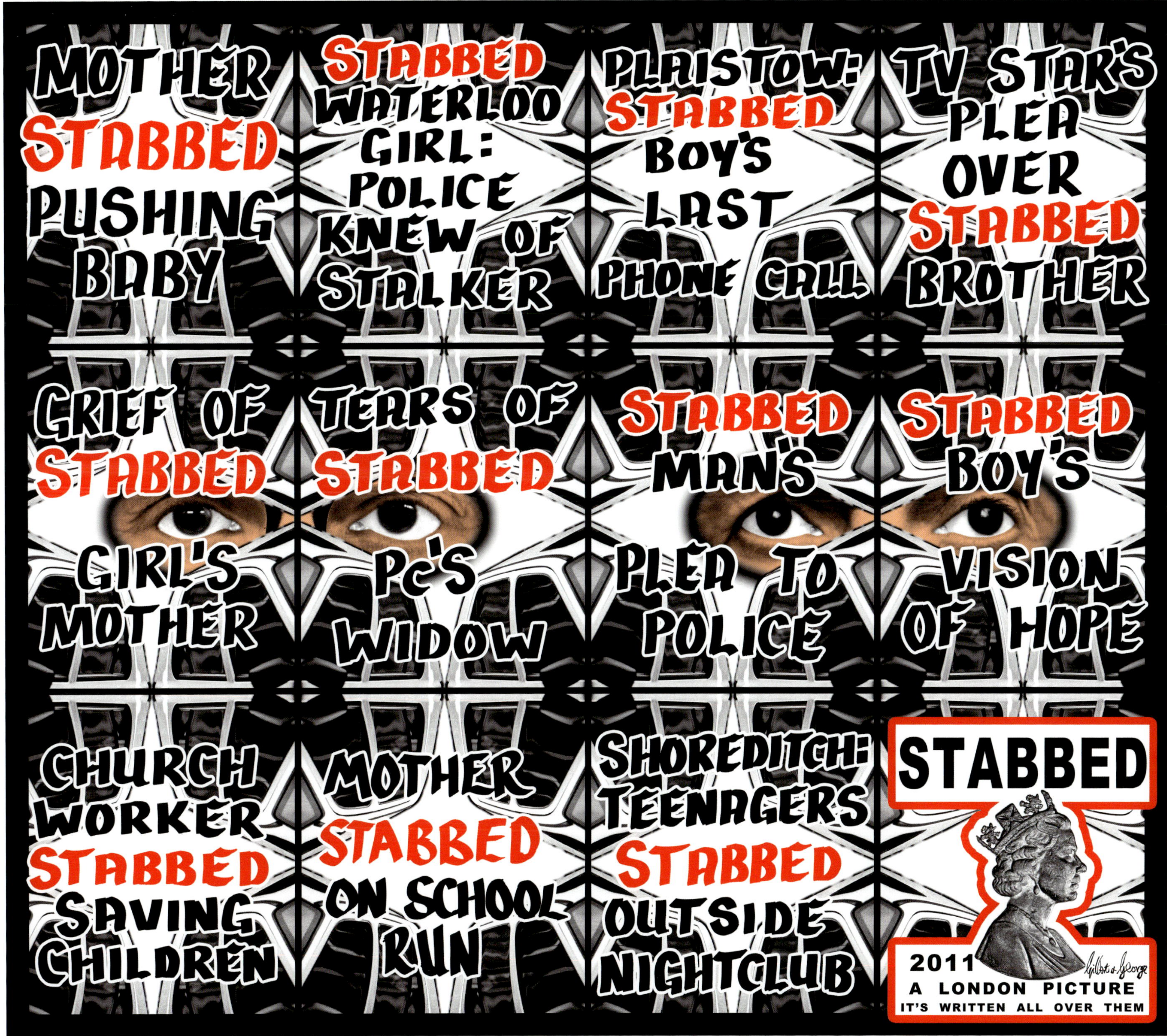

STABBED.   2011.   226 x 254 cm

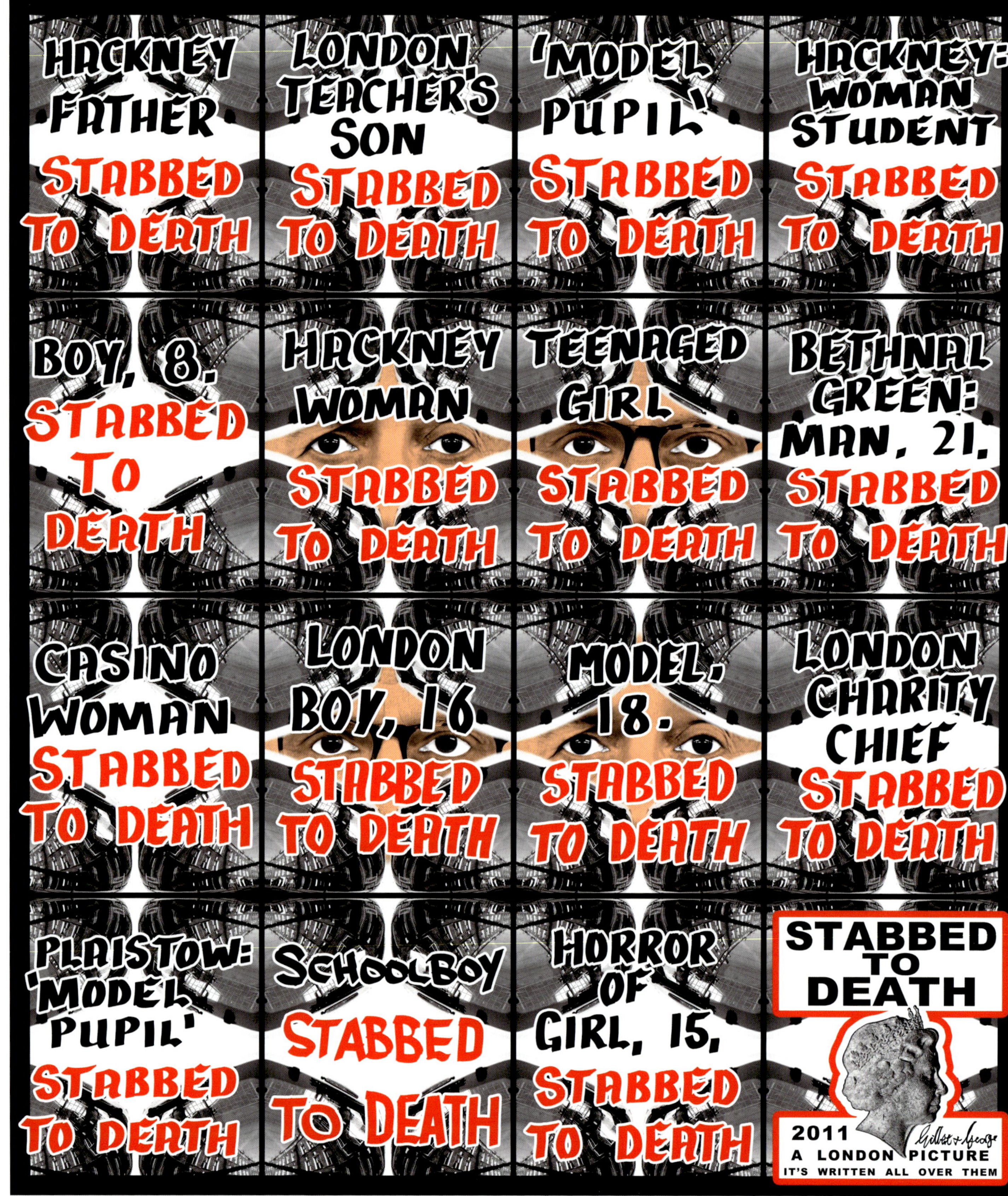

STABBED TO
DEATH

2011

302 x 254 cm

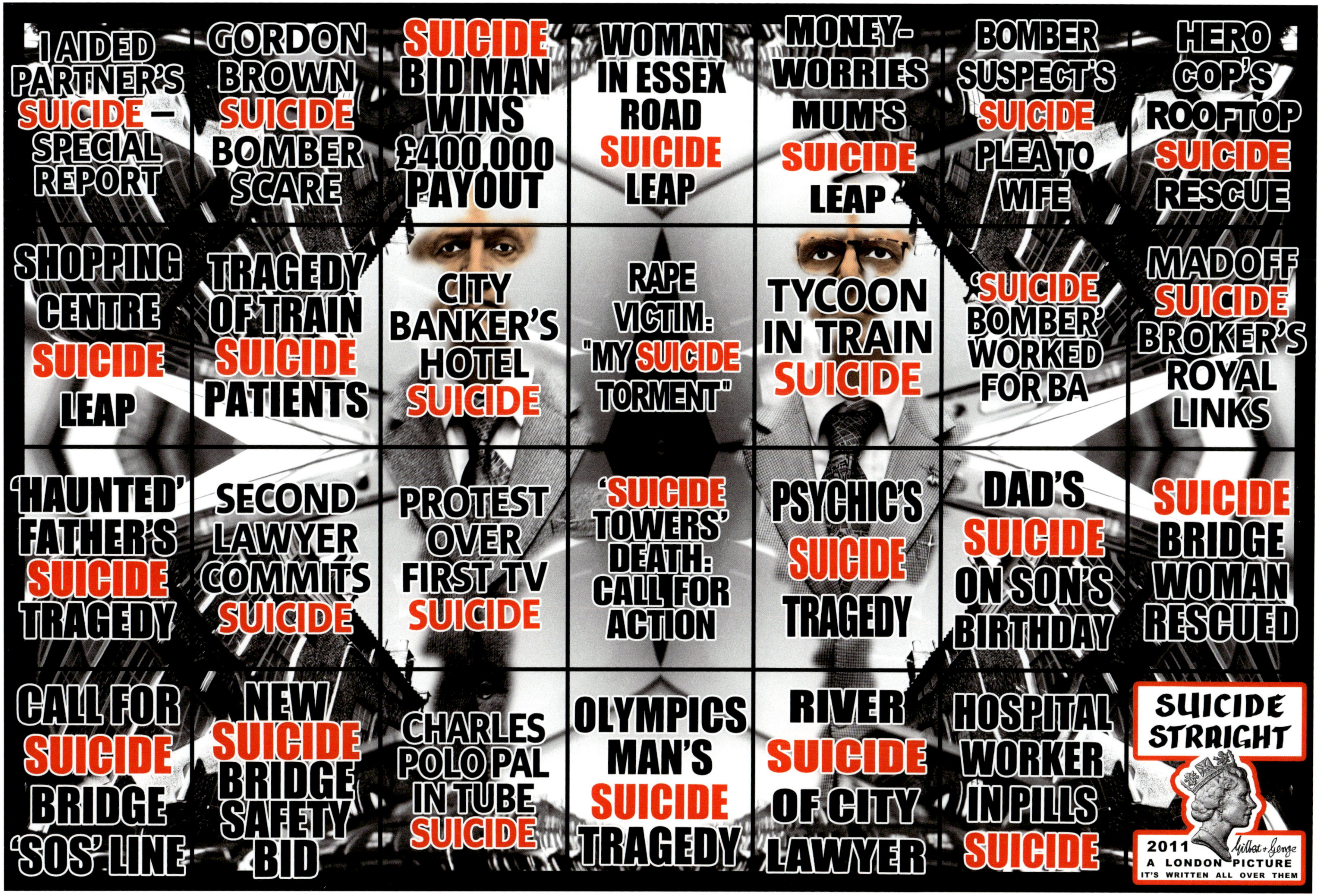

I AIDED PARTNER'S SUICIDE – SPECIAL REPORT

GORDON BROWN SUICIDE BOMBER SCARE

SUICIDE BID MAN WINS £400,000 PAYOUT

WOMAN IN ESSEX ROAD SUICIDE LEAP

MONEY-WORRIES MUM'S SUICIDE LEAP

BOMBER SUSPECT'S SUICIDE PLEA TO WIFE

HERO COP'S ROOFTOP SUICIDE RESCUE

SHOPPING CENTRE SUICIDE LEAP

TRAGEDY OF TRAIN SUICIDE PATIENTS

CITY BANKER'S HOTEL SUICIDE

RAPE VICTIM: "MY SUICIDE TORMENT"

TYCOON IN TRAIN SUICIDE

'SUICIDE BOMBER' WORKED FOR BA

MADOFF SUICIDE BROKER'S ROYAL LINKS

'HAUNTED' FATHER'S SUICIDE TRAGEDY

SECOND LAWYER COMMITS SUICIDE

PROTEST OVER FIRST TV SUICIDE

'SUICIDE TOWERS' DEATH: CALL FOR ACTION

PSYCHIC'S SUICIDE TRAGEDY

DAD'S SUICIDE ON SON'S BIRTHDAY

SUICIDE BRIDGE WOMAN RESCUED

CALL FOR SUICIDE BRIDGE 'SOS' LINE

NEW SUICIDE BRIDGE SAFETY BID

CHARLES POLO PAL IN TUBE SUICIDE

OLYMPICS MAN'S SUICIDE TRAGEDY

RIVER SUICIDE OF CITY LAWYER

HOSPITAL WORKER IN PILLS SUICIDE

SUICIDE STRAIGHT
2011
A LONDON PICTURE
IT'S WRITTEN ALL OVER THEM
Gilbert & George

SUICIDE STRAIGHT.   2011.   302 x 444 cm

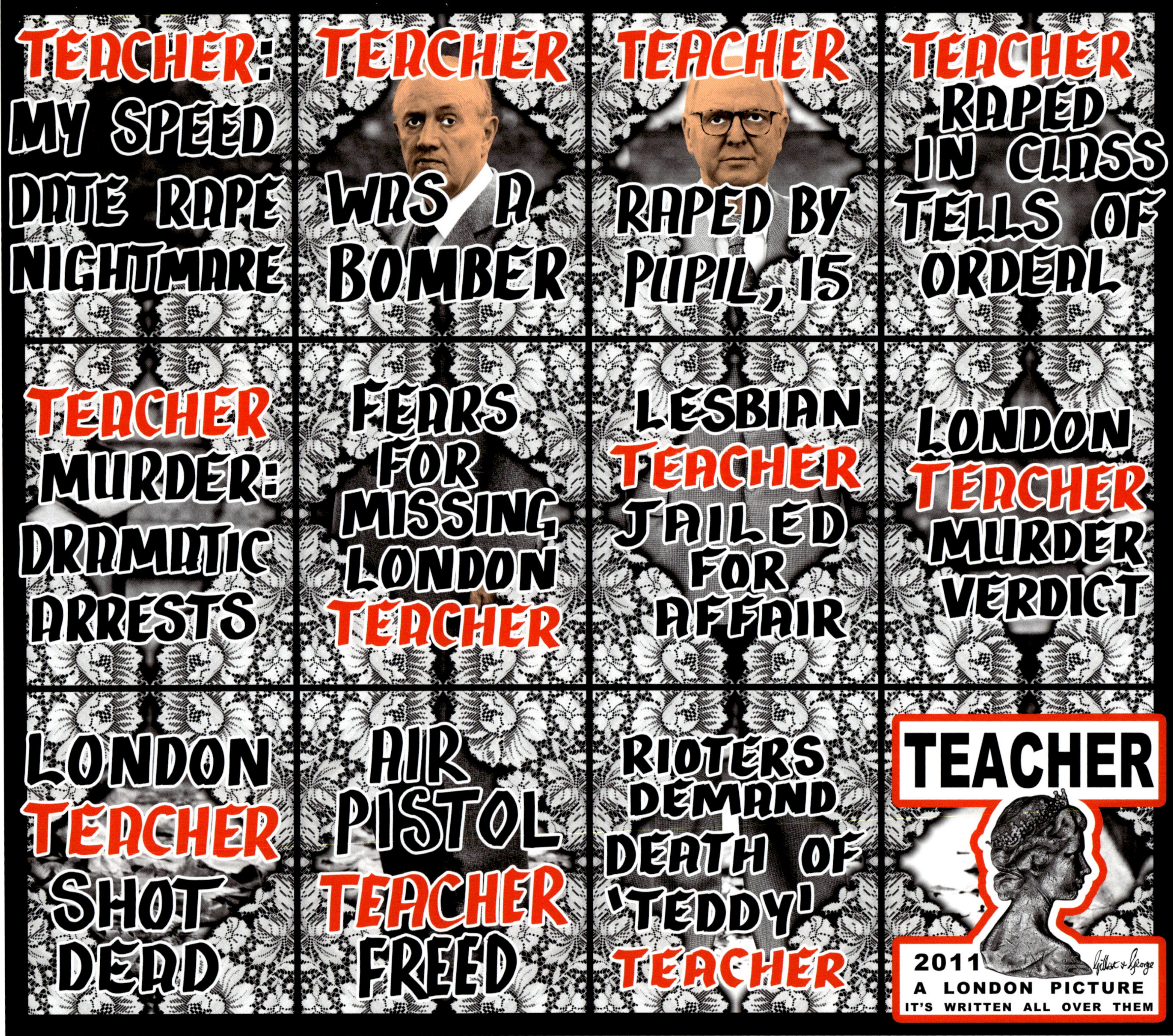

TEACHER.   2011.   226 x 254 cm

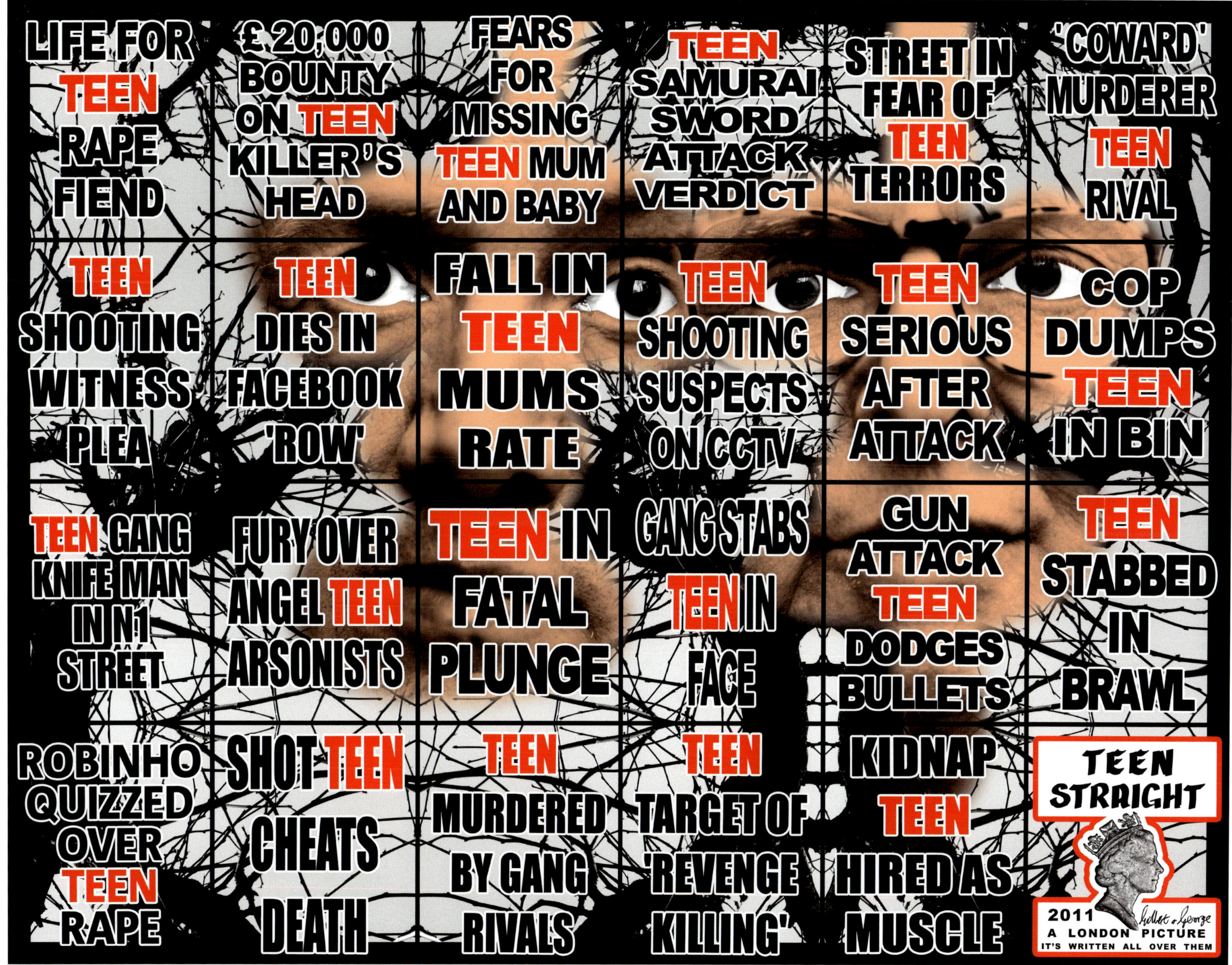

TEEN STRAIGHT.   2011.   302 x 381 cm

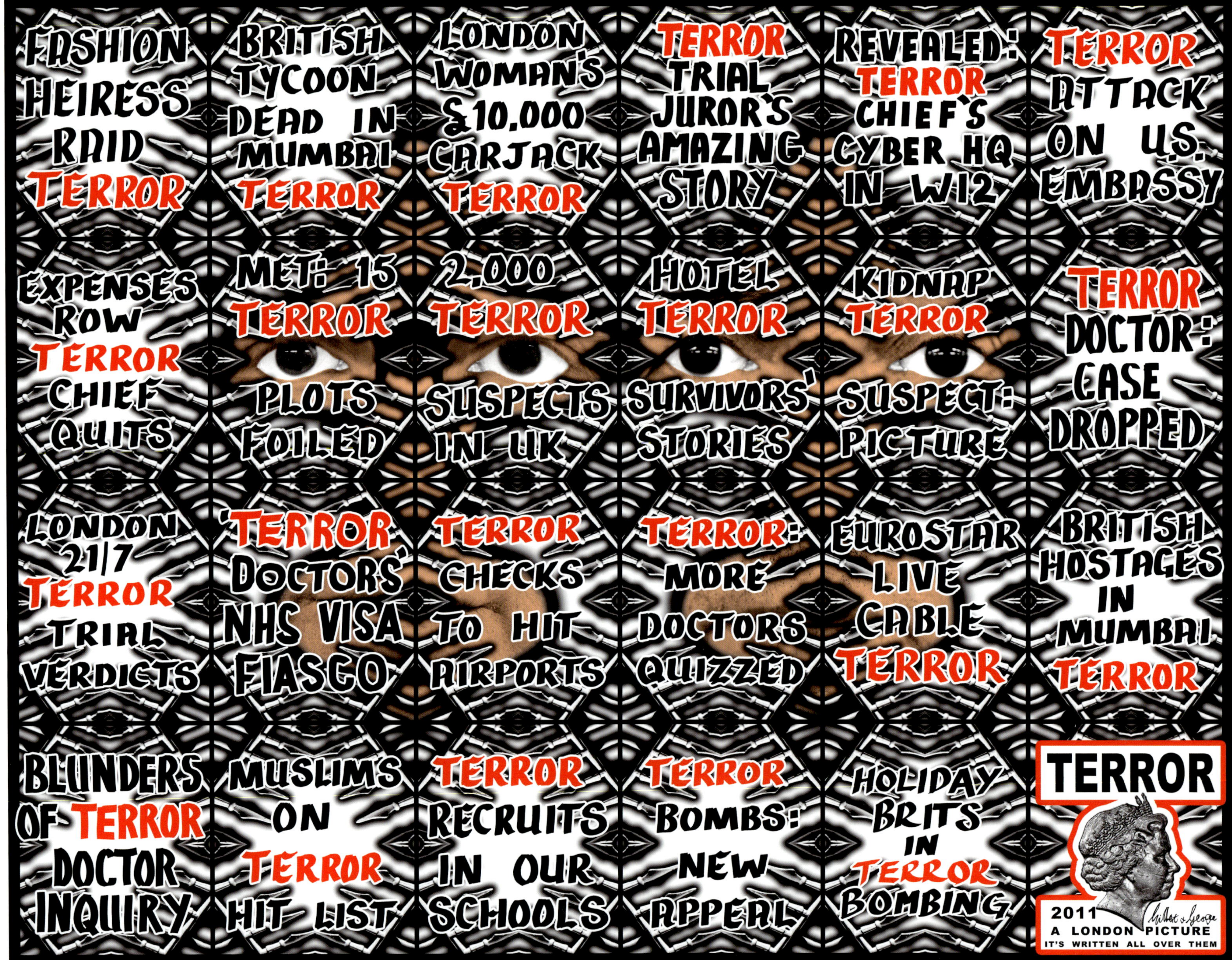

TERROR.   2011.   302 x 381 cm

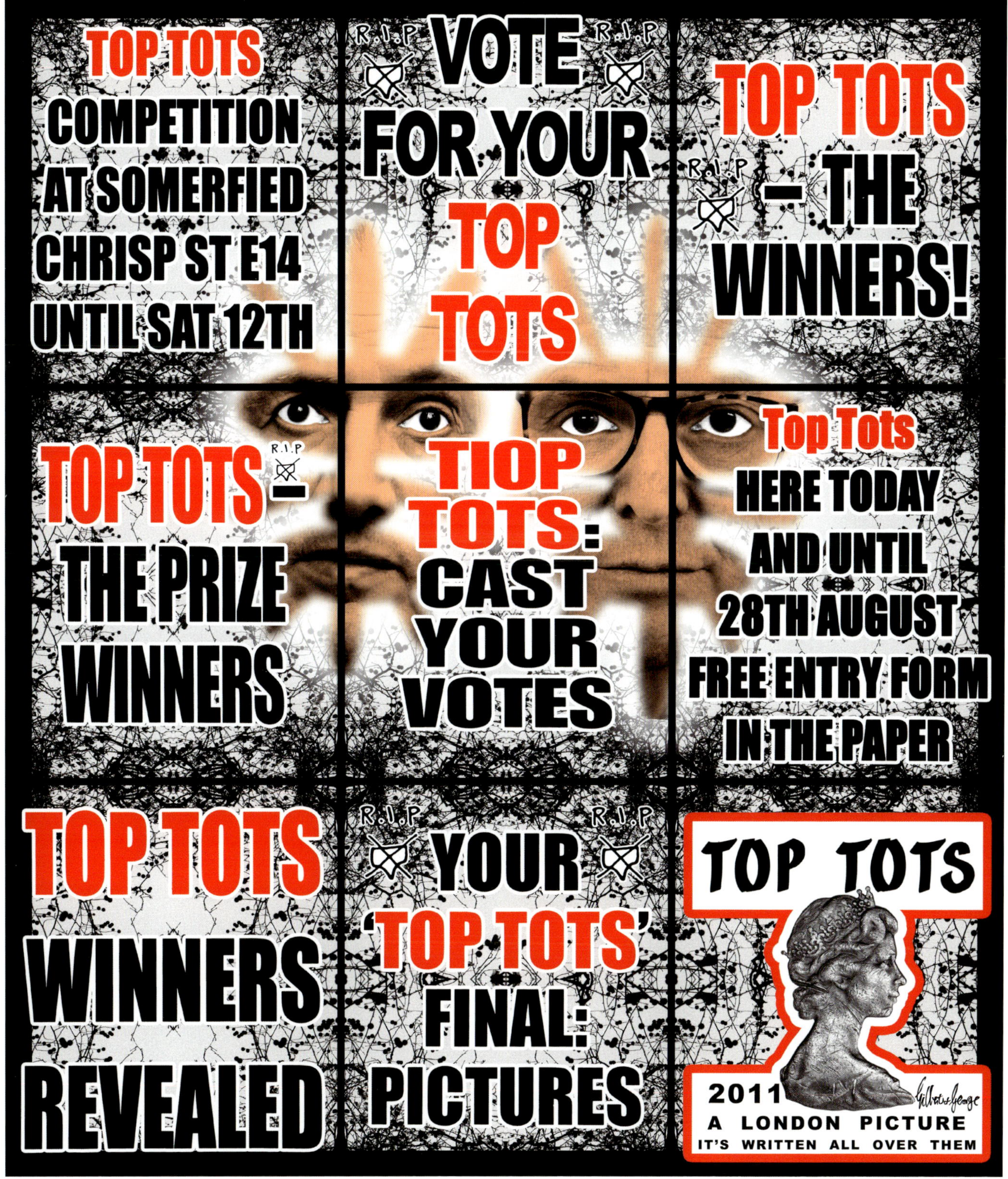

TOP TOTS.   2011.   226 x 190 cm

MUSEUM AND PUBLIC GALLERY EXHIBITIONS 1971 to 2024

1971	THE PAINTINGS	Whitechapel Art Gallery, London
1971	THE PAINTINGS	Stedelijk Museum, Amsterdam
1971	THE PAINTINGS	Kunstverein, Düsseldorf
1972	THE PAINTINGS	Koninklijk Museum, Antwerp
1972	THE PAINTINGS	Kunstmuseum, Luzern
1973	THE SHRUBBERIES & SINGING SCULPTURE	National Gallery of NSW (J. Kaldor proj.), Sydney
1973	THE SHRUBBERIES & SINGING SCULPTURE	National Gallery (J. Kaldor proj.), Melbourne
1976	THE GENERAL JUNGLE	Albright-Knox Gallery, Buffalo
1978	PHOTO-PIECES	Dartington Hall Gallery, Dartington
1980	PHOTO-PIECES 1971 – 1980	Van Abbemuseum, Eindhoven
1981	PHOTO-PIECES 1971 – 1980	Kunsthalle, Düsseldorf
1981	PHOTO-PIECES 1971 – 1980	Kunsthalle, Bern
1981	PHOTO-PIECES 1971 – 1980	Pompidou Centre, Paris
1981	PHOTO-PIECES 1971 – 1980	Whitechapel Art Gallery, London
1981	16TH BIENAL DE SAO PAULO	São Paulo
1982	NEW PHOTO-PIECES	Geward, Gent
1984	GILBERT & GEORGE	The Baltimore Museum of Art, Baltimore
1984	GILBERT & GEORGE	Contemporary Arts Museum, Houston
1984	GILBERT & GEORGE	Norton Gallery, West Palm Beach, Florida
1985	GILBERT & GEORGE	Milwaukee Art Museum, Milwaukee
1985	GILBERT & GEORGE	Guggenheim Museum, New York
1986	PICTURES 1982 – 1985	CAPC, Bordeaux
1986	CHARCOAL ON PAPER SCULPTURES 1970 – 1974	CAPC, Bordeaux
1986	THE PAINTINGS 1971	The Fruitmarket, Edinburgh
1986	PICTURES 1982 – 1985	Kunsthalle, Basel
1986	PICTURES 1982 – 1985	Palais des Beaux-Arts, Brussels
1987	PICTURES 1982 – 1985	Palacio de Velázquez, Madrid
1987	PICTURES 1982 – 1985	Lenbachaus, Munich
1987	PICTURES 1982 – 1985	The Hayward Gallery, London
1987	THE 1986 PICTURES	Aldrich Museum, Ridgefield
1990	PICTURES 1983 – 1988	Central House of the Artists, Moscow
1991	THE COSMOLOGICAL PICTURES	Pałac Sztuki, Krakow
1991	THE COSMOLOGICAL PICTURES	Palazzo delle Esposizioni, Rome
1992	THE COSMOLOGICAL PICTURES	Kunsthalle, Zürich
1992	THE COSMOLOGICAL PICTURES	Wiener Secession, Vienna
1992	THE COSMOLOGICAL PICTURES	Ernst Múzeum, Budapest
1992	THE COSMOLOGICAL PICTURES	Haags Gemeentemuseum, The Hague
1992	NEW DEMOCRATIC PICTURES	Aarhus Kunstmuseum, Aarhus
1992	THE COSMOLOGICAL PICTURES	Irish Museum of Modern Art, Dublin
1992	THE COSMOLOGICAL PICTURES	Fundació Joan Miró, Barcelona
1993	THE COSMOLOGICAL PICTURES	Tate Gallery, Liverpool
1993	THE COSMOLOGICAL PICTURES	Württembergischer Kunstverein, Stuttgart
1993	GILBERT & GEORGE CHINA EXHIBITION	National Art Gallery, Beijing
1993	GILBERT & GEORGE CHINA EXHIBITION	The Art Museum, Shanghai
1994	RETROSPECTIVE	Museo d'Arte Moderna, Lugano
1994	SHITTY NAKED HUMAN WORLD	Wolfsburg Kunstmuseum, Wolfsburg
1995	THE NAKED SHIT PICTURES	South London Gallery, London
1996	THE NAKED SHIT PICTURES	Stedelijk Museum, Amsterdam
1996	GILBERT & GEORGE RETROSPECTIVE	Galleria d'Arte Moderna, Bologna
1997	GILBERT & GEORGE RETROSPECTIVE	Sezon Museum, Tokyo
1997	PICTURES 1991 – 1996	Magasin 3, Stockholm
1997	GILBERT & GEORGE RETROSPECTIVE	Musée d'Art Moderne de la Ville, Paris
1998	NEW TESTAMENTAL PICTURES	Museo di Capodimonte, Naples
1999	GILBERT & GEORGE 1970 – 1988	Astrup Fearnley Museet, Oslo
1999	PICTURES 1986 – 1997	Drassanes, Valencia
1999	PICTURES 1991 – 1997	Ormeau Baths Gallery, Belfast
1999	THE RUDIMENTARY PICTURES	Milton Keynes Gallery, Milton Keynes
1999	NINETEEN NINETY NINE	Kunstmuseum, Bonn
2000	NINETEEN NINETY NINE	Museum Moderner Kunst, Vienna
2000	NINETEEN NINETY NINE	Museum of Contemporary Art, Chicago
2000	MM 2000, BIENNALE DE LYON	Halle Tony Garnier, Lyon
2001	GILBERT & GEORGE	Château d'Arenthon, Alex
2001	THE ART OF GILBERT & GEORGE	The Factory, Athens School of Art, Athens
2002	THE DIRTY WORDS PICTURES	Serpentine Gallery, London
2002	NINE DARK PICTURES	Portikus, Frankfurt
2002	GILBERT & GEORGE	Centro Cultural de Belém, Lisbon
2002	GILBERT & GEORGE	Kunsthaus Bregenz, Austria
2004	TWENTY LONDON EAST ONE PICTURES	Musée d'Art Moderne, Saint-Etienne
2005	GINKGO PICTURES	Venice Biennale, Venice
2005	TWENTY LONDON EAST ONE PICTURES	Kestnergesellschaft, Hanover
2006	SONOFAGOD PICTURES: Was Jesus Heterosexual?	Bonnefanten Museum, Maastricht
2007	MAJOR EXHIBITION	Tate Modern, London
2007	MAJOR EXHIBITION	Haus der Kunst, Munich
2007	MAJOR EXHIBITION	Castello di Rivoli, Turin
2008	MAJOR EXHIBITION	Milwaukee Art Museum, Milwaukee
2008	MAJOR EXHIBITION	De Young Museum, San Francisco
2008	MAJOR EXHIBITION	Brooklyn Museum, New York
2008	NOTATIONS: GILBERT AND GEORGE	Philadelphia Museum of Art, Philadelphia
2010	JACK FREAK PICTURES	Centro de Arte Contemporăneo, Malaga
2010	JACK FREAK PICTURES	Museum of Contemporary Art, Zagreb
2010	THE PAINTINGS (WITH US IN NATURE) 1971	Kröller-Müller Museum, Otterlo
2010	JACK FREAK PICTURES	The Centre for Fine Arts, Brussels
2011	JACK FREAK PICTURES	Deichtorhallen, Hamburg
2011	JACK FREAK PICTURES	Lentos Art Museum, Linz
2011	THE URETHRA POSTCARD PICTURES	Ivorypress Art + Books, Madrid
2011	JACK FREAK PICTURES	Łaźnia Centre for Contemporary Art, Gdańsk
2011	THE URETHRA POSTCARD PICTURES	Pinacotela Giovanni e Marella Agnelli, Turin
2013	LONDON PICTURES	Museum Küppersmühle, Duisburg
2013	LONDON PICTURES	Casal Solleric, Palma
2014	A FAMILY COLLECTION	NMNM – Villa Paloma, Monaco
2015	GILBERT & GEORGE: THE EARLY YEARS	MOMA, New York
2015	GILBERT & GEORGE: THE ART EXHIBITION	MONA, Tasmania
2017	THE SCAPEGOATING PICTURES BERLIN	St. Matthäus Church, Berlin
2017	SCAPEGOATING PICTURES	Ludwig Museum, Budapest
2018	SCAPEGOATING PICTURES	The MAC, Belfast
2018	THE GREAT EXHIBITION	LUMA, Arles
2018	GILBERT & GEORGE MAJOR EXHIBITION	HAM, Helsinki
2019	THE GREAT EXHIBITION	Moderna Museet, Stockholm
2019	THE GREAT EXHIBITION	Astrup Fearnley Museet, Oslo
2020	THE GREAT EXHIBITION	LUMA Westbau + Kunsthalle Zürich, Zürich
2020	THE LOCARNO EXHIBITION	Pinacoteca Comunale Casa Rusca, Locarno
2020	THE GREAT EXHIBITION	Reykjavik Art Museum, Iceland
2021	THE GREAT EXHIBITION	Schirn Kunsthalle, Frankfurt
2022	THE AUCKLAND EXHIBITION	Auckland Art Gallery, New Zealand
2023	THE PARADISICAL PICTURES	Gilbert & George Centre, London

INDEX TO LONDON PICTURE TITLES

Published to accompany the exhibition at

THE GILBERT AND GEORGE CENTRE

5a Heneage Street, London E1 5LJ

LONDON PICTURES
LONDON 2024

HURTWOOD

Published by Hurtwood Press, SB113, 100 Black Prince Road, London SE1 7SJ

ISBN 978-0-903696-89-0

Printed and bound in Great Britain

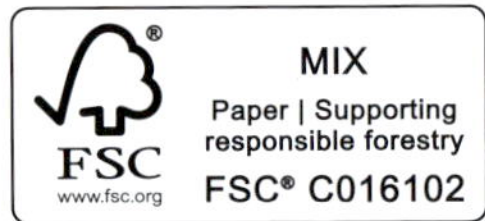

THE GILBERT AND GEORGE CENTRE

www.gilbertandgeorgecentre.org